Covenant
for the
New Millennium

The Beijing Declaration
&
PLATFORM FOR ACTION

from the
FOURTH WORLD CONFERENCE ON WOMEN
Beijing, September 4-15, 1995

FREE ✋ HAND ✋ BOOKS
Santa Rosa, California

This edition contains pages 1-135 of
United Nations Document No. A/CONF.177/20   17 Octo▮
Report of the Fourth World Conference on Women
(Beijing, 4-15 September 1995)

The United Nations Department for Policy Coordination and
Sustainable Development (DPCSD) has made the Report of the
Fourth World Conference on Women available on the Internet
World Wide Web.   The URL is
http://www.undp.org/fwcw/daw1.htm

The text for this printed edition was downloaded from
gopher://gopher.undp.org:70/100/undocs/gad/A/C.

The cover art is the logo of the FWCW and was scanned from the
cover of the Catalogue of Publications for the Fourth World
Conference on Women

ISBN: 0-9651800-0-X

January, 1996
March, 1996

FREE 🖐 HAND 🖐 BOOKS

Santa Rosa, California

Orders to
P.O. Box 184
Tomales, CA 94971
For discounts on multiple copies,
call toll-free 1-800-548-6682
or email fhb@wco.com

Table of Contents

Preface

This edition of the United Nations *Report of the Fourth World Conference on Women*, Beijing, 4-15 September, 1995 was originally prepared for the use of students in courses about the conference taught at Santa Rosa Junior College and Sonoma State University by Tam Stevenson in the Spring Semester, 1996. It has now become a convenient "citizens' edition used by groups and communities following up on the work of the conference.

In the culmination of the Fourth World Conference on Women on September 15, 1995, the representatives of 189 countries voted to adopt *The Beijing Declaration and Platform for Action* and it is that part of the Report which is included here. *The Beijing Declaration* is a magnificent vision for a world we all want to live in and the *Platform for Action* is the practical, specific, and comprehensive directive for bringing it about. These documents represent the historic achievement of women from all over the globe joining together to forthrightly name the twelve *"Critical Areas of Concern"* and describe *"Actions to be Taken"* at all government levels and in the private sector to implement *"the goals of equality, development and peace for all women everywhere and in the interest of all humanity."*

No summary can substitute for the document itself. *The Beijing Declaration* and the *Platform for Action* need to be read, discussed and widely known. In Beijing, 189 governments committed themselves, as governments, to implement the *Platform of Action*. It is now up to the citizenry to join together to enable that implementation. This edition is intended as a step toward that goal.

The chapters in the Report describing the attendance, organization of the work, reports from committees, exchange of views, as well as the Statements of Reservations, are not printed here in order to keep the cost to a minimum. However, the full text of the *Report of the Fourth World Conference on Women* and related resources have been made available on the Internet. They can be found at the following URL:

http://www.undp.org/fwcw/daw1.htm

or by following the links from the U.N. page at

http://www.un.org/

Readers unfamiliar with the World Wide Web on the Internet are encouraged to go to the library to ask for assistance in finding these websites and perhaps thereby discover, as did women attending the conference, the opportunity the Internet provides for global communication and exchange. As someone who followed the conference at home through the websites and electronic listservs — at first with passing interest and then with riveted attention — I can attest to the effectiveness of the use of the Internet by the conference. As reports arrived, including the detailed ENB bulletin with its momentous cadence reporting issues "unbracketed" over and over again, the historic significance of the event, the palpable compassion and transforming power of "Seeing the World through Women's Eyes," brought home to this web novice the sense that the world is forever changed by the Women of Beijing.

There is nothing original in this edition. Both the text and the beautiful cover graphic, which is used on the FWCW web pages, belong to the United Nations. The present text, dated 17 October, 1995, with number A/CONF.177/20 is the final version of the Report of the Fourth World Conference on Women and is currently available at:

gopher://gopher.undp.org:70/100/unconfs/women/off/a--20.en

There is no copyright and dissemination is encouraged, with acknowledgment to the United Nations Department for Policy Coordination and Sustainable Development.

Without the expertise and encouragement of Rick Wonneberger and the patient and generous assistance of Tina Marinics at Lithocraft, this "user friendly" format of the UN Report could not have seen the light of day. Without the enthusiasm for this edition which Patsy Daniels, President of Soroptimist International, has shared with colleagues just about everywhere, very few people would know about it. To the students at Santa Rosa Junior College I owe the certitude of the importance of getting these documents into the hands of citizens everywhere.

JoAnne Black
Santa Rosa Junior College Library
March 8, 1996

The BEIJING DECLARATION

1. We, the Governments participating in the Fourth World Conference on Women,

2. Gathered here in Beijing in September *1995*, the year of the fiftieth anniversary of the founding of the United Nations,

3. Determined to advance the goals of equality, development and peace for all women everywhere in the interest of all humanity,

4. Acknowledging the voices of all women everywhere and taking note of the diversity of women and their roles and circumstances, honoring the women who paved the way and inspired by the hope present in the world's youth,

5. Recognize that the status of women has advanced in some important respects in the past decade but that progress has been uneven, inequalities between women and men have persisted and major obstacles remain, with serious consequences for the well-being of all people,

6. Also recognize that this situation is exacerbated by the increasing poverty that is affecting the lives of the majority of the world's people, in particular women and children, with origins in both the national and international domains,

7. Dedicate ourselves unreservedly to addressing these constraints and obstacles and thus enhancing further the advancement and empowerment of women all over the world, and agree that this requires urgent action in the spirit of determination, hope, cooperation and solidarity, now and to carry us forward into the next century.

We reaffirm our commitment to:

8. The equal rights and inherent human dignity of women and men and other purposes and principles enshrined in the Charter of the United Nations, to the Universal Declaration of Human Rights and other international human rights instruments, in particular the Convention on the Elimination of All Forms of Discrimination against Women and the Convention on the Rights of the Child, as well as the *Declaration on the Elimination of Violence against Women* and the *Declaration on the Right to Development*;

9. Ensure the full implementation of the human rights of women and of the girl child as an inalienable, integral and indivisible part of all human rights and fundamental freedoms;

10. Build on consensus and progress made at previous United Nations conferences and summits - on women in Nairobi in *1985*, on children in New York in *1990*, on environment and development in Rio de Janeiro in *1992*, on human rights in Vienna in *1993*, on population and development in Cairo in *1994* and on social development in Copenhagen in *1995* with the objective of achieving equality, development and peace;

11. Achieve the full and effective implementation of the Nairobi *Forwardlooking Strategies for the Advancement of Women;*

12. The empowerment and advancement of women, including the right to freedom of thought, conscience, religion and belief, thus contributing to the moral, ethical, spiritual and intellectual needs of women and men, individually or in community with others and thereby guaranteeing them the possibility of realizing their full potential in society and shaping their lives in accordance with their own aspirations.

We are convinced that:

13. Women's empowerment and their full participation on the basis of equality in all spheres of society, including participation in the decision-making process and access to power, are fundamental for the achievement of equality, development and peace;

14. Women's rights are human rights;

15. Equal rights, opportunities and access to resources, equal sharing of responsibilities for the family by men and women, and a harmonious partnership between them are critical to their well-being and that of their families as well as to the consolidation of democracy;

16. Eradication of poverty based on sustained economic growth, social development, environmental protection and social justice requires the involvement of women in economic and social development, equal opportunities and the full and equal participation of women and men as agents and beneficiaries of people-centered sustainable development;

17. The explicit recognition and reaffirmation of the right of all women to control all aspects of their health, in particular their own fertility, is basic to their empowerment;

18. Local, national, regional and global peace is attainable and is inextricably linked with the advancement of women, who are a fundamental force for leadership, conflict resolution and the promotion of lasting peace at all levels;

19. It is essential to design, implement and monitor, with the full participation of women, effective, efficient and mutually reinforcing gender-sensitive policies and programs, including development policies and programs, at all levels that will foster the empowerment and advancement of women;

20. The participation and contribution of all actors of civil society, particularly women's groups and networks and other organizations and community-based organizations, with full respect for their autonomy, in cooperation with Governments, are important to the effective implementation and follow-up of the PLATFORM FOR ACTION;

21. The implementation of the PLATFORM FOR ACTION requires commitment from Governments and the international community. By making national and international commitments for action, including those made at the Conference, Governments and the international community recognize the need to take priority action for the empowerment and advancement of women.

We are determined to:

22. Intensify efforts and actions to achieve the goals of the Nairobi *Forwardlooking Strategies for the Advancement of Women* by the end of this century;

23. Ensure the full enjoyment by women and the girl child of all human rights and fundamental freedoms and take effective action against violations of these rights and freedoms;

24. Take all necessary measures to eliminate all forms of discrimination against women and the girl child and remove all obstacles to gender equality and the advancement and empowerment of women;

25. Encourage men to participate fully in all actions towards equality;

26. Promote women's economic independence, including employment, and eradicate the persistent and increasing burden of poverty on women by addressing the structural causes of poverty through changes in economic structures, ensuring equal access for all women, including those in rural areas, as vital development agents, to productive resources, opportunities and public services;

27. Promote people-centered sustainable development, including sustained economic growth, through the provision of basic education, life-long education, literacy and training, and primary health care for girls and women;

28. Take positive steps to ensure peace for the advancement of women and, recognizing the leading role that women have played in the peace movement, work actively towards general and complete disarmament under strict and effective international control, and support negotiations on the conclusion, without delay, of a universal and multilaterally and effectively verifiable comprehensive nuclear-test-ban treaty which contributes to nuclear disarmament and the prevention of the proliferation of nuclear weapons in all its aspects;

29. Prevent and eliminate all forms of violence against women and girls;

30. Ensure equal access to and equal treatment of women and men in education and health care and enhance women's sexual and reproductive health as well as education;

31. Promote and protect all human rights of women and girls;

32. Intensify efforts to ensure equal enjoyment of all human rights and fundamental freedoms for all women and girls who face multiple barriers to their empowerment and advancement because of such factors as their race, age, language, ethnicity, culture, religion, or disability, or because they are indigenous people;

33. Ensure respect for international law, including humanitarian law, in order to protect women and girls in particular;

34. Develop the fullest potential of girls and women of all ages, ensure their full and equal participation in building a better world for all and enhance their role in the development process.

We are determined to:

35. Ensure women's equal access to economic resources, including land, credit, science and technology, vocational training, information, communication and markets, as a means to further the advancement and empowerment of women and girls, including through the enhancement of their capacities to enjoy the benefits of equal access to these resources, *inter alia*, by means of international cooperation;

36. Ensure the success of the PLATFORM FOR ACTION, which will require a strong commitment on the part of Governments, international organizations and institutions at all levels. We are deeply convinced that economic development, social development and environmental protection are interdependent and mutually reinforcing components of sustainable development, which is the framework for our efforts to achieve a higher quality of life for all people. Equitable social development that recognizes empowering the poor, particularly women living in poverty, to utilize environmental resources sustainably is a necessary foundation for sustainable development. We also recognize that broad-based and sustained economic growth in the context of sustainable development is necessary to sustain social development and social justice. The

success of the PLATFORM FOR ACTION will also require adequate mobilization of resources at the national and international levels as well as new and additional resources to the developing countries from all available funding mechanisms, including multilateral, bilateral and private sources for the advancement of women; financial resources to strengthen the capacity of national, subregional, regional and international institutions; a commitment to equal rights, equal participation of women and men in all national, regional and international bodies and policy-making processes; and the establishment or strengthening of mechanisms at all levels for accountability to the world's women;

37. Ensure also the success of the PLATFORM FOR ACTION in countries with economies in transition, which will require continued international cooperation and assistance;

38. We hereby adopt and commit ourselves as Governments to implement the following PLATFORM FOR ACTION, ensuring that a gender perspective is reflected in all our policies and programs. We urge the United Nations system, regional and international financial institutions, other relevant regional and international institutions and all women and men, as well as non-governmental organizations, with full respect for their autonomy, and all sectors of civil society, in cooperation with Governments, to fully commit themselves and contribute to the implementation of this PLATFORM FOR ACTION.

PLATFORM FOR ACTION

Chapter I

Mission Statement

1. The PLATFORM FOR ACTION is an agenda for women's empowerment. It aims at accelerating the implementation of the Nairobi *Forward-looking Strategies for the Advancement of Women*[1] and at removing all the obstacles to women's active participation in all spheres of public and private life through a full and equal share in economic, social, cultural and political decision-making. This means that the principle of shared power and responsibility should be established between women and men at home, in the workplace and in the wider national and international communities. Equality between women and men is a matter of human rights and a condition for social justice and is also a necessary and fundamental prerequisite for equality, development and peace. A transformed partnership based on equality between women and men is a condition for people-centered sustainable development. A sustained and long-term commitment is essential, so that women and men can work together for themselves, for their children and for society to meet the challenges of the twenty-first century.

2. The PLATFORM FOR ACTION reaffirms the fundamental principle set forth in the Vienna *Declaration and Program of Action*,[2] adopted by the World Conference on Human Rights, that the human rights of women and of the girl child are an inalienable, integral and indivisible part of universal human rights. As an agenda for action, the Platform seeks to promote and protect the full enjoyment of all human rights and the fundamental freedoms of all women throughout their life cycle.

3. The PLATFORM FOR ACTION emphasizes that women share common concerns that can be addressed only by working together and in partnership with men towards the common goal of gender* equality around the world. It respects and values the full diversity of

women's situations and conditions and recognizes that some women face particular barriers to their empowerment.

4. The PLATFORM FOR ACTION requires immediate and concerted action by all to create a peaceful, just and humane world based on human rights and fundamental freedoms, including the principle of equality for all people of all ages and from all walks of life, and to this end, recognizes that broadbased and sustained economic growth in the context of sustainable development is necessary to sustain social development and social justice.

5. The success of the PLATFORM FOR ACTION will require a strong commitment on the part of Governments, international organizations and institutions at all levels. It will also require adequate mobilization of resources at the national and international levels as well as new and additional resources to the developing countries from all available funding mechanisms, including multilateral, bilateral and private sources for the advancement of women; financial resources to strengthen the capacity of national, subregional, regional and international institutions; a commitment to equal rights, equal responsibilities and equal opportunities and to the equal participation of women and men in all national, regional and international bodies and policy-making processes; and the establishment or strengthening of mechanisms at all levels for accountability to the world's women.

* Annexes I-IV are to be issued as an addendum to this Report. Annex IV is the *Statement by the President of the Conference on the Commonly Understood Meaning of the Term "Gender."*[As they become available, these Annexes will be found on the Internet at this URL: http://www.undp.org/fwcw/daw1.htm]

Chapter II

Global Framework

6. The FOURTH WORLD CONFERENCE ON WOMEN is taking place as the world stands poised on the threshold of a new millennium.

7. The PLATFORM FOR ACTION upholds the Convention on the Elimination of All Forms of Discrimination against Women[3] and builds upon the *Nairobi Forward-looking Strategies for the Advancement of Women*, as well as relevant resolutions adopted by the Economic and Social Council and the General Assembly. The formulation of the PLATFORM FOR ACTION is aimed at establishing a basic group of priority actions that should be carried out during the next five years.

8. The PLATFORM FOR ACTION recognizes the importance of the agreements reached at the World Summit for Children, the United Nations Conference on Environment and Development, the World Conference on Human Rights, the International Conference on Population and Development and the World Summit for Social Development, which set out specific approaches and commitments to fostering sustainable development and international cooperation and to strengthening the role of the United Nations to that end. Similarly, the Global Conference on the Sustainable Development of Small Island Developing States, the International Conference on Nutrition, the International Conference on Primary Health Care and the World Conference on Education for All have addressed the various facets of development and human rights, within their specific perspectives, paying significant attention to the role of women and girls. In addition, the International Year for the World's Indigenous People,[4] the International Year of the Family,[5] the United Nations Year for Tolerance,[6] the Geneva *Declaration for Rural Women*,[7] and the *Declaration on the Elimination of Violence against Women*[8] have also emphasized the issues of women's empowerment and equality.

9. The objective of the PLATFORM FOR ACTION, which is in full conformity with the purposes and principles of the Charter of the United Nations and international law, is the empowerment of all women. The full realization of all human rights and fundamental freedoms of all women is essential for the empowerment of women. While the significance of national and regional particularities and various historical, cultural and religious backgrounds must be borne in mind, it is the duty of States, regardless of their political,

economic and cultural systems, to promote and protect all human rights and fundamental freedoms.[9] The implementation of this Platform, including through national laws and the formulation of strategies, policies, programs and development priorities, is the sovereign responsibility of each State, in conformity with all human rights and fundamental freedoms, and the significance of and full respect for various religious and ethical values, cultural backgrounds and philosophical convictions of individuals and their communities should contribute to the full enjoyment by women of their human rights in order to achieve equality, development and peace.

10. Since the World Conference to Review and Appraise the Achievements of the United Nations Decade for Women: Equality, Development and Peace, held at Nairobi in 1985, and the adoption of the Nairobi *Forward-looking Strategies for the Advancement of Women,* the world has experienced profound political, economic, social and cultural changes, which have had both positive and negative effects on women. The World Conference on Human Rights recognized that the human rights of women and the girl child are an inalienable, integral and indivisible part of universal human rights. The full and equal participation of women in political, civil, economic, social and cultural life at the national, regional and international levels, and the eradication of all forms of discrimination on the grounds of sex are priority objectives of the international community. The World Conference on Human Rights reaffirmed the solemn commitment of all States to fulfill their obligations to promote universal respect for, and observance and protection of, all human rights and fundamental freedoms for all in accordance with the Charter of the United Nations, other instruments related to human rights and international law. The universal nature of these rights and freedoms is beyond question.

11. The end of the cold war has resulted in international changes and diminished competition between the super-Powers. The threat of a global armed conflict has diminished, while international relations have improved and prospects for peace among nations have increased. Although the threat of global conflict has been reduced, wars of aggression, armed conflicts, colonial or other forms of alien domination and foreign occupation, civil wars, and terrorism continue to plague many parts of the world. Grave violations of the human rights of women occur, particularly in times of armed conflict, and include murder, torture, systematic rape, forced pregnancy and forced abortion, in particular under policies of ethnic cleansing.

12. The maintenance of peace and security at the global, regional and local levels, together with the prevention of policies of aggression and ethnic cleansing and the resolution of armed conflict, is crucial for the protection of the human rights of women and girl children, as well as for the elimination of all forms of violence against them and of their use as a weapon of war.

13. Excessive military expenditures, including global military expenditures and arms trade or trafficking, and investments for arms production and acquisition have reduced the resources available for social development. As a result of the debt burden and other economic difficulties, many developing countries have undertaken structural adjustment policies. Moreover, there are structural adjustment programs that have been poorly designed and implemented, with resulting detrimental effects on social development. The number of people living in poverty has increased disproportionately in most developing countries, particularly the heavily indebted countries, during the past decade.

14. In this context, the social dimension of development should be emphasized. Accelerated economic growth, although necessary for social development, does not by itself improve the quality of life of the population. In some cases, conditions can arise which can aggravate social inequality and marginalization. Hence, it is indispensable to search for new alternatives that ensure that all members of society benefit from economic growth based on a holistic approach to all aspects of development: growth, equality between women and men, social justice, conservation and protection of the environment, sustainability, solidarity, participation, peace and respect for human rights.

15. A world-wide movement towards democratization has opened up the political process in many nations, but the popular participation of women in key decision-making as full and equal partners with men, particularly in politics, has not yet been achieved. South Africa's policy of institutionalized racism apartheid - has been dismantled and a peaceful and democratic transfer of power has occurred. In Central and Eastern Europe the transition to parliamentary democracy has been rapid and has given rise to a variety of experiences, depending on the specific circumstances of each country. While the transition has been mostly peaceful, in some countries this process has been hindered by armed conflict that has resulted in grave violations of human rights.

16. Widespread economic recession, as well as political instability in some regions, has been responsible for setting back development goals in many countries. This has led to the expansion of unspeakable poverty. Of the more than 1 billion people living in abject

poverty, women are an overwhelming majority. The rapid process of change and adjustment in all sectors has also led to increased unemployment and underemployment, with particular impact on women. In many cases, structural adjustment programs have not been designed to minimize their negative effects on vulnerable and disadvantaged groups or on women, nor have they been designed to assure positive effects on those groups by preventing their marginalization in economic and social activities. The Final Act of the Uruguay Round of multilateral trade negotiations[10] underscored the increasing interdependence of national economies, as well as the importance of trade liberalization and access to open, dynamic markets. There has also been heavy military spending in some regions. Despite increases in official development assistance (ODA) by some countries, ODA has recently declined overall.

17. Absolute poverty and the feminization of poverty, unemployment, the increasing fragility of the environment, continued violence against women and the widespread exclusion of half of humanity from institutions of power and governance underscore the need to continue the search for development, peace and security and for ways of assuring people-centered sustainable development. The participation and leadership of the half of humanity that is female is essential to the success of that search. Therefore, only a new era of international cooperation among Governments and peoples based on a spirit of partnership, an equitable, international social and economic environment, and a radical transformation of the relationship between women and men to one of full and equal partnership will enable the world to meet the challenges of the twenty-first century.

18. Recent international economic developments have had in many cases a disproportionate impact on women and children, the majority of whom live in developing countries. For those States that have carried a large burden of foreign debt, structural adjustment programs and measures, though beneficial in the long term, have led to a reduction in social expenditures, thereby adversely affecting women, particularly in Africa and the least developed countries. This is exacerbated when responsibilities for basic social services have shifted from Governments to women.

19. Economic recession in many developed and developing countries, as well as ongoing restructuring in countries with economies in transition, have had a disproportionately negative impact on women's employment. Women often have no choice but to take employment that lacks long-term job security or involves dangerous working conditions, to work in unprotected home-based production or to be unemployed. Many women enter the labor market

in under-remunerated and undervalued jobs, seeking to improve their household income; others decide to migrate for the same purpose. Without any reduction in their other responsibilities, this has increased the total burden of work for women.

20. Macro and micro-economic policies and programs, including structural adjustment, have not always been designed to take account of their impact on women and girl children, especially those living in poverty. Poverty has increased in both absolute and relative terms, and the number of women living in poverty has increased in most regions. There are many urban women living in poverty; however, the plight of women living in rural and remote areas deserves special attention given the stagnation of development in such areas. In developing countries, even those in which national indicators have shown improvement, the majority of rural women continue to live in conditions of economic underdevelopment and social marginalization. 21. Women are key contributors to the economy and to combating poverty through both remunerated and unremunerated work at home, in the community and in the workplace. Growing numbers of women have achieved economic independence through gainful employment.

22. One fourth of all households world wide are headed by women and many other households are dependent on female income even where men are present. Female maintained households are very often among the poorest because of wage discrimination, occupational segregation patterns in the labor market and other gender-based barriers. Family disintegration, population movements between urban and rural areas within countries, international migration, war and internal displacements are factors contributing to the rise of female-headed households.

23. Recognizing that the achievement and maintenance of peace and security are a precondition for economic and social progress, women are increasingly establishing themselves as central actors in a variety of capacities in the movement of humanity for peace. Their full participation in decisionmaking, conflict prevention and resolution and all other peace initiatives is essential to the realization of lasting peace.

24. Religion, spirituality and belief play a central role in the lives of millions of women and men, in the way they live and in the aspirations they have for the future. The right to freedom of thought, conscience and religion is inalienable and must be universally enjoyed. This right includes the freedom to have or to adopt the religion or belief of their choice either individually or in community with others, in public or in private, and to manifest their religion or belief in worship, observance, practice and teaching. In order to re-

alize equality, development and peace, there is a need to respect these rights and freedoms fully. Religion, thought, conscience and belief may, and can, contribute to fulfilling women's and men's moral, ethical and spiritual needs and to realizing their full potential in society. However, it is acknowledged that any form of extremism may have a negative impact on women and can lead to violence and discrimination.

25. The FOURTH WORLD CONFERENCE ON WOMEN should accelerate the process that formally began in 1975, which was proclaimed International Women's Year by the United Nations General Assembly. The Year was a turning-point in that it put women's issues on the agenda. The United Nations Decade for Women (1976-1985) was a world-wide effort to examine the status and rights of women and to bring women into decision-making at all levels. In 1979, the General Assembly adopted the Convention on the Elimination of All Forms of Discrimination against Women, which entered into force in 1981 and set an international standard for what was meant by equality between women and men. In 1985, the World Conference to Review and Appraise the Achievements of the United Nations Decade for Women: Equality, Development and Peace adopted the Nairobi *Forward-looking Strategies for the Advancement of Women*, to be implemented by the year 2000. There has been important progress in achieving equality between women and men. Many Governments have enacted legislation to promote equality between women and men and have established national machineries to ensure the mainstreaming of gender perspectives in all spheres of society. International agencies have focused greater attention on women's status and roles.

26. The growing strength of the non-governmental sector, particularly women's organizations and feminist groups, has become a driving force for change. Non-governmental organizations have played an important advocacy role in advancing legislation or mechanisms to ensure the promotion of women. They have also become catalysts for new approaches to development. Many Governments have increasingly recognized the important role that non governmental organizations play and the importance of working with them for progress. Yet, in some countries, Governments continue to restrict the ability of non-governmental organizations to operate freely. Women, through non-governmental organizations, have participated in and strongly influenced community, national, regional and global forums and international debates.

27. Since 1975, knowledge of the status of women and men, respectively, has increased and is contributing to further actions aimed at promoting equality between women and men. In several countries,

there have been important changes in the relationships between women and men, especially where there have been major advances in education for women and significant increases in their participation in the paid labor force. The boundaries of the gender division of labor between productive and reproductive roles are gradually being crossed as women have started to enter formerly male dominated areas of work and men have started to accept greater responsibility for domestic tasks, including child care. However, changes in women's roles have been greater and much more rapid than changes in men's roles. In many countries, the differences between women's and men's achievements and activities are still not recognized as the consequences of socially constructed gender roles rather than immutable biological differences.

28. Moreover, 10 years after the Nairobi Conference, equality between women and men has still not been achieved. On average, women represent a mere 10 per cent of all elected legislators world wide and in most national and international administrative structures, both public and private, they remain underrepresented. The United Nations is no exception. Fifty years after its creation, the United Nations is continuing to deny itself the benefits of women's leadership by their underrepresentation at decision making levels within the Secretariat and the specialized agencies.

29. Women play a critical role in the family. The family is the basic unit of society and as such should be strengthened. It is entitled to receive comprehensive protection and support. In different cultural, political and social systems, various forms of the family exist. The rights, capabilities and responsibilities of family members must be respected. Women make a great contribution to the welfare of the family and to the development of society, which is still not recognized or considered in its full importance. The social significance of maternity, motherhood and the role of parents in the family and in the upbringing of children should be acknowledged. The upbringing of children requires shared responsibility of parents, women and men and society as a whole. Maternity, motherhood, parenting and the role of women in procreation must not be a basis for discrimination nor restrict the full participation of women in society. Recognition should also be given to the important role often played by women in many countries in caring for other members of their family.

30. While the rate of growth of world population is on the decline, world population is at an all-time high in absolute numbers, with current increments approaching 86 million persons annually. Two other major demographic trends have had profound repercussions on the dependency ratio within families. In many developing

countries, 45 to 50 per cent of the population is less than 15 years old, while in industrialized nations both the number and proportion of elderly people are increasing. According to United Nations projections, 72 per cent of the population over 60 years of age will be living in developing countries by the year 2025, and more than half of that population will be women. Care of children, the sick and the elderly is a responsibility that falls disproportionately on women, owing to lack of equality and the unbalanced distribution of remunerated and unremunerated work between women and men.

31. Many women face particular barriers because of various diverse factors in addition to their gender. Often these diverse factors isolate or marginalize such women. They are, inter alia, denied their human rights, they lack access or are denied access to education and vocational training, employment, housing and economic self-sufficiency and they are excluded from decision-making processes. Such women are often denied the opportunity to contribute to their communities as part of the mainstream.

32. The past decade has also witnessed a growing recognition of the distinct interests and concerns of indigenous women, whose identity, cultural traditions and forms of social organization enhance and strengthen the communities in which they live. Indigenous women often face barriers both as women and as members of indigenous communities.

33. In the past 20 years, the world has seen an explosion in the field of communications. With advances in computer technology and satellite and cable television, global access to information continues to increase and expand, creating new opportunities for the participation of women in communications and the mass media and for the dissemination of information about women. However, global communication networks have been used to spread stereotyped and demeaning images of women for narrow commercial and consumerist purposes. Until women participate equally in both the technical and decision-making areas of communications and the mass media, including the arts, they will continue to be misrepresented and awareness of the reality of women's lives will continue to be lacking. The media have a great potential to promote the advancement of women and the equality of women and men by portraying women and men in a non-stereotypical, diverse and balanced manner, and by respecting the dignity and worth of the human person.

34. The continuing environmental degradation that affects all human lives has often a more direct impact on women. Women's health and their livelihood are threatened by pollution and toxic wastes, large-scale deforestation, desertification, drought and depletion of the soil and of coastal and marine resources, with a rising incidence of envi-

ronmentally related health problems and even death reported among women and girls. Those most affected are rural and indigenous women, whose livelihood and daily subsistence depends directly on sustainable ecosystems.

35. Poverty and environmental degradation are closely interrelated. While poverty results in certain kinds of environmental stress, the major cause of the continued deterioration of the global environment is the unsustainable patterns of consumption and production, particularly in industrialized countries, which are a matter of grave concern and aggravate poverty and imbalances.

36. Global trends have brought profound changes in family survival strategies and structures. Rural to urban migration has increased substantially in all regions. The global urban population is projected to reach 47 per cent of the total population by the year 2000. An estimated 125 million people are migrants, refugees and displaced persons, half of whom live in developing countries. These massive movements of people have profound consequences for family structures and well-being and have unequal consequences for women and men, including in many cases the sexual exploitation of women.

37. According to World Health Organization (WHO) estimates, by the beginning of 1995 the number of cumulative cases of acquired immunodeficiency syndrome (AIDS) was 4.5 million. An estimated 19.5 million men, women and children have been infected with the human immunodeficiency virus (HIV) since it was first diagnosed and it is projected that another 20 million will be infected by the end of the decade. Among new cases, women are twice as likely to be infected as men. In the early stage of the AIDS pandemic, women were not infected in large numbers; however, about 8 million women are now infected. Young women and adolescents are particularly vulnerable. It is estimated that by the year 2000 more than 13 million women will be infected and 4 million women will have died from AIDS-related conditions. In addition, about 250 million new cases of sexually transmitted diseases are estimated to occur every year. The rate of transmission of sexually transmitted diseases, including HIV/AIDS, is increasing at an alarming rate among women and girls, especially in developing countries.

38. Since 1975, significant knowledge and information have been generated about the status of women and the conditions in which they live. Throughout their entire life cycle, women's daily existence and long-term aspirations are restricted by discriminatory attitudes, unjust social and economic structures, and a lack of resources in most countries that prevent their full and equal participation. In a number of countries, the practice of prenatal sex selec-

tion, higher rates of mortality among very young girls and lower rates of school enrollment for girls as compared with boys suggest that son preference is curtailing the access of girl children to food, education and health care and even life itself. Discrimination against women begins at the earliest stages of life and must therefore be addressed from then onwards.

39. The girl child of today is the woman of tomorrow. The skills, ideas and energy of the girl child are vital for full attainment of the goals of equality, development and peace. For the girl child to develop her full potential she needs to be nurtured in an enabling environment, where her spiritual, intellectual and material needs for survival, protection and development are met and her equal rights safeguarded. If women are to be equal partners with men, in every aspect of life and development, now is the time to recognize the human dignity and worth of the girl child and to ensure the full enjoyment of her human rights and fundamental freedoms, including the rights assured by the Convention on the Rights of the Child,[1] universal ratification of which is strongly urged. Yet there exists world-wide evidence that discrimination and violence against girls begin at the earliest stages of life and continue unabated throughout their lives. They often have less access to nutrition, physical and mental health care and education and enjoy fewer rights, opportunities and benefits of childhood and adolescence than do boys. They are often subjected to various forms of sexual and economic exploitation, pedophilia, forced prostitution and possibly the sale of their organs and tissues, violence and harmful practices such as female infanticide and prenatal sex selection, incest, female genital mutilation and early marriage, including child marriage.

40. Half the world's population is under the age of 25 and most of the world's youth - more than 85 per cent - live in developing countries. Policy makers must recognize the implications of these demographic factors. Special measures must be taken to ensure that young women have the life skills necessary for active and effective participation in all levels of social, cultural, political and economic leadership. It will be critical for the international community to demonstrate a new commitment to the future - a commitment to inspiring a new generation of women and men to work together for a more just society. This new generation of leaders must accept and promote a world in which every child is free from injustice, oppression and inequality and free to develop her/his own potential. The principle of equality of women and men must therefore be integral to the socialization process.

Chapter III

Critical Areas Of Concern

41. The advancement of women and the achievement of equality between women and men are a matter of human rights and a condition for social justice and should not be seen in isolation as a women's issue. They are the only way to build a sustainable, just and developed society. Empowerment of women and equality between women and men are prerequisites for achieving political, social, economic, cultural and environmental security among all peoples.

42. Most of the goals set out in the Nairobi *Forward-looking Strategies for the Advancement of Women* have not been achieved. Barriers to women's empowerment remain, despite the efforts of Governments, as well as non governmental organizations and women and men everywhere. Vast political, economic and ecological crises persist in many parts of the world. Among them are wars of aggression, armed conflicts, colonial or other forms of alien domination or foreign occupation, civil wars and terrorism. These situations, combined with systematic or de facto discrimination, violations of and failure to protect all human rights and fundamental freedoms of all women, and their civil, cultural, economic, political and social rights, including the right to development and ingrained prejudicial attitudes towards women and girls are but a few of the impediments encountered since the World Conference to Review and Appraise the Achievements of the United Nations Decade for Women: Equality, Development and Peace, in 1985.

43. A review of progress since the Nairobi Conference highlights special concerns - areas of particular urgency that stand out as priorities for action. All actors should focus action and resources on the strategic objectives relating to the critical areas of concern which are, necessarily, interrelated, interdependent and of high priority. There is a need for these actors to develop and implement mechanisms of accountability for all the areas of concern.

44. To this end, Governments, the international community and civil society, including non-governmental organizations and the private sector, are called upon to take strategic action in the following critical areas of concern:

THE CRITICAL AREAS OF CONCERN

1. The persistent and increasing burden of poverty on women

2. Inequalities and inadequacies in and unequal access to education and training

3. Inequalities and inadequacies in, and unequal access to health care and related services

4. Violence against women

5. The effects of armed or other kinds of conflict on women, including those living under foreign occupation

6. Inequality in economic structures and policies, in all forms of productive activities and in access to resources

7. Inequality between men and women in the sharing of power and decision-making at all levels

8. Insufficient mechanisms at all levels to promote the advancement of women

9. Lack of respect for and inadequate promotion and protection of the human rights of women

10. Stereotyping of women and inequality in women's access to and participation in all communication systems, especially in the media

11. Gender inequalities in the management of natural resources and in the safeguarding of the environment

12. Persistent discrimination against and violation of the rights of the girl child.

Chapter IV

Strategic Objectives and Actions

45. In each critical area of concern, the problem is diagnosed and strategic objectives are proposed with concrete actions to be taken by various actors in order to achieve those objectives. The strategic objectives are derived from the critical areas of concern and specific actions to be taken to achieve them cut across the boundaries of equality, development and peace - the goals of the *Nairobi Forward-looking Strategies for the Advancement of Women* - and reflect their interdependence. The objectives and actions are interlinked, of high priority and mutually reinforcing. The PLATFORM FOR ACTION is intended to improve the situation of all women, without exception, who often face similar barriers, while special attention should be given to groups that are the most disadvantaged.

46. The PLATFORM FOR ACTION recognizes that women face barriers to full equality and advancement because of such factors as their race, age, language, ethnicity, culture, religion or disability, because they are indigenous women or because of other status. Many women encounter specific obstacles related to their family status, particularly as single parents; and to their socio-economic status, including their living conditions in rural, isolated or impoverished areas. Additional barriers also exist for refugee women, other displaced women, including internally displaced women as well as for immigrant women and migrant women, including women migrant workers. Many women are also particularly affected by environmental disasters, serious and infectious diseases and various forms of violence against women.

Chapter IV. A

WOMEN AND POVERTY

47. More than 1 billion people in the world today, the great majority of whom are women, live in unacceptable conditions of poverty, mostly in the developing countries. Poverty has various causes, including structural ones. Poverty is a complex, multidimensional problem, with origins in both the national and international domains. The globalization of the world's economy and the deepening interdependence among nations present challenges and oppor-

tunities for sustained economic growth and development, as well as risks and uncertainties for the future of the world economy. The uncertain global economic climate has been accompanied by economic restructuring as well as, in a certain number of countries, persistent, unmanageable levels of external debt and structural adjustment programs In addition, all types of conflict, displacement of people and environmental degradation have undermined the capacity of Governments to meet the basic needs of their populations. Transformations in the world economy are profoundly changing the parameters of social development in all countries. One significant trend has been the increased poverty of women, the extent of which varies from region to region. The gender disparities in economic power-sharing are also an important contributing factor to the poverty of women. Migration and consequent changes in family structures have placed additional burdens on women, especially those who provide for several dependents.

Macroeconomic policies need rethinking and reformulation to address such trends. These policies focus almost exclusively on the formal sector. They also tend to impede the initiatives of women and fail to consider the differential impact on women and men. The application of gender analysis to a wide range of policies and programs is therefore critical to poverty reduction strategies. In order to eradicate poverty and achieve sustainable development, women and men must participate fully and equally in the formulation of macroeconomic and social policies and strategies for the eradication of poverty.

The eradication of poverty cannot be accomplished through anti-poverty programs alone but will require democratic participation and changes in economic structures in order to ensure access for all women to resources, opportunities and public services. Poverty has various manifestations, including lack of income and productive resources sufficient to ensure a sustainable livelihood; hunger and malnutrition; ill health; limited or lack of access to education and other basic services; increasing morbidity and mortality from illness; homelessness and inadequate housing; unsafe environments; and social discrimination and exclusion. It is also characterized by lack of participation in decision-making and in civil, social and cultural life. It occurs in all countries - as mass poverty in many developing countries and as pockets of poverty amidst wealth in developed countries.

Poverty may be caused by an economic recession that results in loss of livelihood or by disaster or conflict. There is also the poverty of low-wage workers and the utter destitution of people who fall outside family support systems, social institutions and safety nets.

48. In the past decade the number of women living in poverty has increased disproportionately to the number of men, particularly in the developing countries. The feminization of poverty has also recently become a significant problem in the countries with economies in transition as a short-term consequence of the process of political, economic and social transformation. In addition to economic factors, the rigidity of socially ascribed gender roles and women's limited access to power, education, training and productive resources as well as other emerging factors that may lead to insecurity for families are also responsible. The failure to adequately mainstream a gender perspective in all economic analysis and planning and to address the structural causes of poverty is also a contributing factor.

49. Women contribute to the economy and to combating poverty through both remunerated and unremunerated work at home, in the community and in the workplace. The empowerment of women is a critical factor in the eradication of poverty.

50. While poverty affects households as a whole, because of the gender division of labor and responsibilities for household welfare, women bear a disproportionate burden, attempting to manage household consumption and production under conditions of increasing scarcity. Poverty is particularly acute for women living in rural households.

51. Women's poverty is directly related to the absence of economic opportunities and autonomy, lack of access to economic resources, including credit, land ownership and inheritance, lack of access to education and support services and their minimal participation in the decision-making process. Poverty can also force women into situations in which they are vulnerable to sexual exploitation.

52. In too many countries, social welfare systems do not take sufficient account of the specific conditions of women living in poverty, and there is a tendency to scale back the services provided by such systems. The risk of falling into poverty is greater for women than for men, particularly in old age, where social security systems are based on the principle of continuous remunerated employment. In some cases, women do not fulfill this requirement because of interruptions in their work, due to the unbalanced distribution of remunerated and unremunerated work. Moreover, older women also face greater obstacles to labor-market re-entry.

53. In many developed countries, where the level of general education and professional training of women and men are similar and where systems of protection against discrimination are available, in some sectors the economic transformations of the past decade have strongly increased either the unemployment of women or the pre-

carious nature of their employment. The proportion of women among the poor has consequently increased. In countries with a high level of school enrollment of girls, those who leave the educational system the earliest, without any qualification, are among the most vulnerable in the labor market.

54. In countries with economies in transition and in other countries undergoing fundamental political, economic and social transformations, these transformations have often led to a reduction in women's income or to women being deprived of income.

55. Particularly in developing countries, the productive capacity of women should be increased through access to capital, resources, credit, land, technology, information, technical assistance and training so as to raise their income and improve nutrition, education, health care and status within the household. The release of women's productive potential is pivotal to breaking the cycle of poverty so that women can share fully in the benefits of development and in the products of their own labor.

56. Sustainable development and economic growth that is both sustained and sustainable are possible only through improving the economic, social, political, legal and cultural status of women. Equitable social development that recognizes empowering the poor, particularly women, to utilize environmental resources sustainably is a necessary foundation for sustainable development.

57. The success of policies and measures aimed at supporting or strengthening the promotion of gender equality and the improvement of the status of women should be based on the integration of the gender perspective in general policies relating to all spheres of society as well as the implementation of positive measures with adequate institutional and financial support at all levels.

STRATEGIC OBJECTIVE A. 1

> *&. Review, adopt and maintain macroeconomic policies and development strategies that address the needs and efforts of women in poverty.*

Actions to be taken

58. By Governments:

   (a) Review and modify, with the full and equal participation of women, macroeconomic and social policies with a view to achieving the objectives of the PLATFORM FOR ACTION ;

   (b) Analyze, from a gender perspective, policies and programs including those related to macroeconomic stability, structural adjustment, external debt problems, taxation, investments, employment, markets and all rele-

vant sectors of the economy - with respect to their impact on poverty, on inequality and particularly on women; assess their impact on family well being and conditions and adjust them, as appropriate, to promote more equitable distribution of productive assets, wealth, opportunities, income and services;

(c) Pursue and implement sound and stable macroeconomic and sectoral policies that are designed and monitored with the full and equal participation of women, encourage broad-based sustained economic growth, address the structural causes of poverty and are geared towards eradicating poverty and reducing gender-based inequality within the overall framework of achieving people-centered sustainable development;

(d) Restructure and target the allocation of public expenditures to promote women's economic opportunities and equal access to productive resources and to address the basic social, educational and health needs of women, particularly those living in poverty;

(e) Develop agricultural and fishing sectors, where and as necessary, in order to ensure, as appropriate, household and national food security and food self-sufficiency, by allocating the necessary financial, technical and human resources;

(f) Develop policies and programs to promote equitable distribution of food within the household;

(g) Provide adequate safety nets and strengthen State-based and community-based support systems, as an integral part of social policy, in order to enable women living in poverty to withstand adverse economic environments and preserve their livelihood, assets and revenues in times of crisis;

(h) Generate economic policies that have a positive impact on the employment and income of women workers in both the formal and informal sectors and adopt specific measures to address women's unemployment, in particular their long-term unemployment;

(i) Formulate and implement, when necessary, specific economic, social, agricultural and related policies in support of female-headed households;

(j) Develop and implement anti-poverty programs, including employment schemes, that improve access to food for women living in poverty, including through the use of appropriate pricing and distribution mechanisms;

(k) Ensure the full realization of the human rights of all women migrants, including women migrant workers, and their protection against violence and exploitation; introduce measures for the empowerment of documented women migrants, including women migrant workers; facilitate the productive employment of documented migrant women through greater recognition of their skills, foreign education and credentials, and facilitate their full integration into the labor force;

(l) Introduce measures to integrate or reintegrate women living in poverty and socially marginalized women into productive employment and the economic mainstream; ensure that internally displaced women have full access

to economic opportunities and that the qualifications and skills of immigrant and refugee women are recognized;

(*m*) Enable women to obtain affordable housing and access to land by, among other things, removing all obstacles to access, with special emphasis on meeting the needs of women, especially those living in poverty and female heads of household;

(*n*) Formulate and implement policies and programs that enhance the access of women agricultural and fisheries producers (including subsistence farmers and producers, especially in rural areas) to financial, technical, extension and marketing services; provide access to and control of land, appropriate infrastructure and technology in order to increase women's incomes and promote household food security, especially in rural areas and, where appropriate, encourage the development of producer-owned, market-based cooperatives;

(*o*) Create social security systems wherever they do not exist, or review them with a view to placing individual women and men on an equal footing, at every stage of their lives;

(*p*) Ensure access to free or low-cost legal services, including legal-literacy, especially designed to reach women living in poverty;

(*q*) Take particular measures to promote and strengthen policies and programs for indigenous women with their full participation and respect for their cultural diversity, so that they have opportunities and the possibility of choice in the development process in order to eradicate the poverty that affects them.

59. By multilateral financial and development institutions, including the World Bank, the International Monetary Fund and regional development institutions, and through bilateral development cooperation:

(*a*) In accordance with the commitments made at the World Summit for Social Development, seek to mobilize new and additional financial resources that are both adequate and predictable and mobilized in a way that maximizes the availability of such resources and uses all available funding sources and mechanisms with a view to contributing towards the goal of poverty eradication and targeting women living in poverty;

(*b*) Strengthen analytical capacity in order to more systematically strengthen gender perspectives and integrate them into the design and implementation of lending programs, including structural adjustment and economic recovery programs;

(*c*) Find effective development-oriented and durable solutions to external debt problems in order to help them to finance programs and projects targeted at development, including the advancement of women, *inter alia*, through the immediate implementation of the terms of debt forgiveness agreed upon in the Paris Club in December 1994, which encompassed debt reduction, including cancellation or other debt relief measures and develop techniques of debt conversion applied to social development programs and projects in conformity with the priorities of the PLATFORM FOR ACTION ;

(d) Invite the international financial institutions to examine innovative-approaches to assisting low-income countries with a high proportion of multilateral debt, with a view to alleviating their debt burden;

(e) Ensure that structural adjustment programs are designed to minimize their negative effects on vulnerable and disadvantaged groups and communities and to assure their positive effects on such groups and communities by preventing their marginalization in economic and social activities and devising measures to ensure that they gain access to and control over economic resources and economic and social activities; take actions to reduce inequality and economic disparity;

(f) Review the impact of structural adjustment programs on social development by means of gender-sensitive social impact assessments and other relevant methods, in order to develop policies to reduce their negative effects and improve their positive impact, ensuring that women do not bear a disproportionate burden of transition costs; complement adjustment lending with enhanced, targeted social development lending;

(g) Create an enabling environment that allows women to build and maintain sustainable livelihoods.

60. By national and international non-governmental organizations and women's groups:

(a) Mobilize all parties involved in the development process, including academic institutions, non-governmental organizations and grass-roots and women's groups, to improve the effectiveness of anti-poverty programs directed towards the poorest and most disadvantaged groups of women, such as rural and indigenous women, female heads of household, young women and older women, refugees and migrant women and women with disabilities, recognizing that social development is primarily the responsibility of Governments;

(b) Engage in lobbying and establish monitoring mechanisms s appropriate, and other relevant activities to ensure implementation of the recommendations on poverty eradication outlined in the PLATFORM FOR ACTION and aimed at ensuring accountability and transparency from the State and private sectors;

(c) Include in their activities women with diverse needs and recognize that youth organizations are increasingly becoming effective partners in development programs;

(d) In cooperation with the government and private sectors, participate in the development of a comprehensive national strategy for improving health, education and social services so that girls and women of all ages living in poverty have full access to such services; seek funding to secure access to services with a gender perspective and to extend those services in order to

reach the rural and remote areas that are not covered by government institutions;

(e) In cooperation with Governments, employers, other social partners and relevant parties, contribute to the development of education and training and retraining policies to ensure that women can acquire a wide range of skills to meet new demands;

(f) Mobilize to protect women's right to full and equal access to economic resources, including the right to inheritance and to ownership of land and other property, credit, natural resources and appropriate technologies.

STRATEGIC OBJECTIVE A.2.

> *Revise laws and administrative practices to ensure women's equal rights and access to economic resources*

Actions to be taken

61. By Governments:

   (a) Ensure access to free or low-cost legal services, including legal literacy, especially designed to reach women living in poverty;

   (b) Undertake legislative and administrative reforms to give women full and equal access to economic resources, including the right to inheritance and to ownership of land and other property, credit, natural resources and appropriate technologies;

   (c) Consider ratification of Convention No. 169 of the International Labour Organization (ILO) as part of their efforts to promote and protect the rights of indigenous people

STRATEGIC OBJECTIVE A.3.

> *Provide women with access to savings and credit mechanisms and institutions*

Actions to be taken

62. By Governments:

   (a) Enhance the access of disadvantaged women, including women entrepreneurs, in rural, remote and urban areas to financial services through strengthening links between the formal banks and intermediary lending organizations, including legislative support, training for women and institutional strengthening for intermediary institutions with a view to mobilizing capital for those institutions and increasing the availability of credit;

   (b) Encourage links between financial institutions and non-governmental organizations and support innovative lending practices, including those that

integrate credit with women's services and training and provide credit facilities to rural women.

63. By commercial banks, specialized financial institutions and the private sector in examining their policies:

(*a*) Use credit and savings methodologies that are effective in reaching women in poverty and innovative in reducing transaction costs and redefining risk;

(*b*) Open special windows for lending to women, including young women, who lack access to traditional sources of collateral;

(*c*) Simplify banking practices, for example by reducing the minimum deposit and other requirements for opening bank accounts;

(*d*) Ensure the participation and joint ownership, where possible, of women clients in the decision-making of institutions providing credit and financial services.

64. By multilateral and bilateral development cooperation organizations: Support, through the provision of capital and/or resources, financial institutions that serve low-income, small-scale and micro-scale women entrepreneurs and producers, in both the formal and informal sectors.

65. By Governments and multilateral financial institutions, as appropriate: Support institutions that meet performance standards in reaching large numbers of low-income women and men through capitalization, refinancing and institutional development support in forms that foster self-sufficiency.

66. By international organizations: Increase funding for programs and projects designed to promote sustainable and productive entrepreneurial activities for income generation among disadvantaged women and women living in poverty.

STRATEGIC OBJECTIVE A.4.

> *Develop gender-based methodologies and conduct research to address the feminization of poverty*

Actions to be taken

67. By Governments, intergovernmental organizations, academic and research institutions and the private sector:

(*a*) Develop conceptual and practical methodologies for incorporating gender perspectives into all aspects of economic policy-making, including structural adjustment planning and programs;

(*b*) Apply these methodologies in conducting gender-impact analyses of all policies and programs, including structural adjustment programs, and disseminate the research findings.

68. By national and international statistical organizations:

  (a) Collect gender and age-desegregated data on poverty and all aspects of economic activity and develop qualitative and quantitative statistical indicators to facilitate the assessment of economic performance from a gender perspective;

  (b) Devise suitable statistical means to recognize and make visible the full extent of the work of women and all their contributions to the national economy, including their contribution in the unremunerated and domestic sectors, and examine the relationship of women's unremunerated work to the incidence of and their vulnerability to poverty.

Chapter IV. B

EDUCATION AND TRAINING OF WOMEN

69. Education is a human right and an essential tool for achieving the goals of equality, development and peace. Non-discriminatory education benefits both girls and boys and thus ultimately contributes to more equal relationships between women and men. Equality of access to and attainment of educational qualifications is necessary if more women are to become agents of change. Literacy of women is an important key to improving health, nutrition and education in the family and to empowering women to participate in decision-making in society. Investing in formal and nonformal education and training for girls and women, with its exceptionally high social and economic return, has proved to be one of the best means of achieving sustainable development and economic growth that is both sustained and sustainable.

70. On a regional level, girls and boys have achieved equal access to primary education, except in some parts of Africa, in particular sub-Saharan Africa, and Central Asia, where access to education facilities is still inadequate. Progress has been made in secondary education, where equal access of girls and boys has been achieved in some countries. Enrollment of girls and women in tertiary education has increased considerably. In many countries, private schools have also played an important complementary role in improving access to education at all levels. Yet, more than five years after the World Conference on Education for All (Jomtien, Thailand, 1990) adopted the World Declaration on Education for All and the Framework for Action to Meet Basic Learning Needs,[12] approximately 100 million children, including at least 60 million girls, are without access to primary schooling and more than two thirds of the world's 960 million illiterate adults are women. The high rate of illiteracy prevailing in most developing countries, in particular in sub-Saharan Africa and some Arab States, remains a severe impediment to the advancement of women and to development.

71. Discrimination in girls' access to education persists in many areas, owing to customary attitudes, early marriages and pregnancies, inadequate and gender-biased teaching and educational materials,

sexual harassment and lack of adequate and physically and otherwise accessible schooling facilities. Girls undertake heavy domestic work at a very early age. Girls and young women are expected to manage both educational and domestic responsibilities, often resulting in poor scholastic performance and early drop-out from the educational system. This has long-lasting consequences for all aspects of women's lives.

72. Creation of an educational and social environment, in which women and men, girls and boys, are treated equally and encouraged to achieve their full potential, respecting their freedom of thought, conscience, religion and belief, and where educational resources promote non-stereotyped images of women and men, would be effective in the elimination of the causes of discrimination against women and inequalities between women and men.

73. Women should be enabled to benefit from an ongoing acquisition of knowledge and skills beyond those acquired during youth. This concept of lifelong learning includes knowledge and skills gained in formal education and training, as well as learning that occurs in informal ways, including volunteer activity, unremunerated work and traditional knowledge.

74 Curricula and teaching materials remain gender-biased to a large degree, and are rarely sensitive to the specific needs of girls and women. This reinforces traditional female and male roles that deny women opportunities for full and equal partnership in society. Lack of gender awareness by educators at all levels strengthens existing inequities between males and females by reinforcing discriminatory tendencies and undermining girls' self-esteem. The lack of sexual and reproductive health education has a profound impact on women and men.

75. Science curricula in particular are gender-biased. Science textbooks do not relate to women's and girls' daily experience and fail to give recognition to women scientists. Girls are often deprived of basic education in mathematics and science and technical training, which provide knowledge they could apply to improve their daily lives and enhance their employment opportunities. Advanced study in science and technology prepares women to take an active role in the technological and industrial development of their countries, thus necessitating a diverse approach to vocational and technical training. Technology is rapidly changing the world and has also affected the developing countries. It is essential that women not only benefit from technology, but also participate in the process from the design to the application, monitoring and evaluation stages.

76. Access for and retention of girls and women at all levels of education, including the higher level, and all academic areas is one of the

factors of their continued progress in professional activities. Nevertheless, it can be noted that girls are still concentrated in a limited number of fields of study.

77. The mass media are a powerful means of education. As an educational tool the mass media can be an instrument for educators and governmental and non-governmental institutions for the advancement of women and for development. Computerized education and information systems are increasingly becoming an important element in learning and the dissemination of knowledge. Television especially has the greatest impact on young people and, as such, has the ability to shape values, attitudes and perceptions of women and girls in both positive and negative ways. It is therefore essential that educators teach critical judgment and analytical skills.

78. Resources allocated to education, particularly for girls and women, are in many countries insufficient and in some cases have been further diminished, including in the context of adjustment policies and programs. Such insufficient resource allocations have a long-term adverse effect on human development, particularly on the development of women.

79. In addressing unequal access to and inadequate educational opportunities, Governments and other actors should promote an active and visible policy of mainstreaming a gender perspective into all policies and programs, so that, before decisions are taken, an analysis is made of the effects on women and men, respectively.

STRATEGIC OBJECTIVE B. 1.

ᴂ *Ensure equal access to education*

Actions to be taken

80. By Governments:

(a) Advance the goal of equal access to education by taking measures to eliminate discrimination in education at all levels on the basis of gender, race, language, religion, national origin, age or disability, or any other form of discrimination and, as appropriate, consider establishing procedures to address grievances;

(b) By the year 2000, provide universal access to basic education and ensure compåletion of primary education by at least 80 per cent of primary school-age children; close the gender gap in primary and secondary school education by the year 2005; provide universal primary education in all countries before the year 2015;

(c) Eliminate gender disparities in access to all areas of tertiary education by ensuring that women have equal access to career development, training, scholarships and fellowships, and by adopting positive action when appropriate;

(d) Create a gender-sensitive educational system in order to ensure equal educational and training opportunities and full and equal participation of women in educational administration and policy- and decision-making;

(e) Provide - in collaboration with parents, non-governmental organizations, including youth organizations, communities and the private sector - young women with academic and technical training, career planning, leadership and social skills and work experience to prepare them to participate fully in society;

(f) Increase enrollment and retention rates of girls by allocating appropriate budgetary resources; by enlisting the support of parents and the community, as well as through campaigns, flexible school schedules, incentives, scholarships and other means to minimize the costs of girls' education to their families and to facilitate parents' ability to choose education for the girl child; and by ensuring that the rights of women and girls to freedom of conscience and religion are respected in educational institutions through repealing any discriminatory laws or legislation based on religion, race or culture;

(g) Promote an educational setting that eliminates all barriers that impeded the schooling of pregnant adolescents and young mothers, including, as appropriate, affordable and physically accessible childcare facilities and parental education to encourage those who are responsible for the care of their children and siblings during their school years, to return to or continue with and complete schooling;

(h) Improve the quality of education and equal opportunities for women and men in terms of access in order to ensure that women of all ages can acquire the knowledge, capacities, aptitudes, skills and ethical values needed to develop and to participate fully under equal conditions in the process of social, economic and political development;

(i) Make available non-discriminatory and gender-sensitive professional school counseling and career education programs to encourage girls to pursue academic and technical curricula in order to widen their future career opportunities;

(j) Encourage ratification of the *International Covenant on Economic, Social and Cultural Rights*[13] where they have not already done so.

STRATEGIC OBJECTIVE B.2.

&ewsp; *Eradicate illiteracy among women*

Actions to be taken

81. By Governments, national, regional and international bodies, bilateral and multilateral donors and non-governmental organizations:

   (a) Reduce the female illiteracy rate to at least half its 1990 level, with emphasis on rural women, migrant, refugee and internally displaced women and women with disabilities;

   (b) Provide universal access to, and seek to ensure gender equality in the completion of, primary education for girls by the year 2000; (c) Eliminate the gender gap in basic and functional literacy, as recommended in the World Declaration on Education for All (Jomtien);

   (d) Narrow the disparities between developed and developing countries;

   (e) Encourage adult and family engagement in learning to promote total literacy for all people;

   (f) Promote, together with literacy, life skills and scientific and technological knowledge and work towards an expansion of the definition of literacy, taking into account current targets and benchmarks.

STRATEGIC OBJECTIVE B.3.

> ❧ *Improve women's access to vocational training, science and technology, and continuing education*

Actions to be taken

82. By Governments, in cooperation with employers, workers and trade unions, international and non-governmental organizations, including women's and youth organizations, and educational institutions:

   (a) Develop and implement education, training and retraining policies for women, especially young women and women re-entering the labor market, to provide skills to meet the needs of a changing socio-economic context for improving their employment opportunities;

   (b) Provide recognition to non-formal educational opportunities for girls and women in the educational system;

   (c) Provide information to women and girls on the availability and benefits of vocational training, training programs in science and technology and programs of continuing education;

   (d) Design educational and training programs for women who are unemployed in order to provide them with new knowledge and skills that will enhance and broaden their employment opportunities, including selfemployment, and development of their entrepreneurial skills;

   (e) Diversify vocational and technical training and improve access for and retention of girls and women in education and vocational training in such fields as science, mathematics, engineering, environmental sciences and technology, information technology and high technology, as well as management training;

(f) Promote women's central role in food and agricultural research, extension and education programs;

(g) Encourage the adaptation of curricula and teaching materials, encourage a supportive training environment and take positive measures to promote training for the full range of occupational choices of non traditional careers for women and men, including the development of multidisciplinary courses for science and mathematics teachers to sensitize them to the relevance of science and technology to women's lives;

(h) Develop curricula and teaching materials and formulate and take positive measures to ensure women better access to and participation in technical and scientific areas, especially areas where they are not represented or are underrepresented;

(i) Develop policies and programs to encourage women to participate in all apprenticeship programs;

(j) Increase training in technical, managerial, agricultural extension and marketing areas for women in agriculture, fisheries, industry and business, arts and crafts, to increase income-generating opportunities, women's participation in economic decision-making, in particular through women's organizations at the grass-roots level, and their contribution to production, marketing, business, and science and technology;

(k) Ensure access to quality education and training at all appropriate levels for adult women with little or no education, for women with disabilities and for documented migrant, refugee and displaced women to improve their work opportunities.

STRATEGIC OBJECTIVE B.4.

> ❧ *Develop non-discriminatory education and training*

Actions to be taken

83. By Governments, educational authorities and other educational and academic institutions:

(a) Elaborate recommendations and develop curricula, textbooks and teaching aids free of gender-based stereotypes for all levels of education, including teacher training, in association with all concerned - publishers, teachers, public authorities and parents' associations;

(b) Develop training programs and materials for teachers and educators that raise awareness about the status, role and contribution of women and men in the family, as defined in paragraph 29 above, and society; in this context, promote equality, cooperation, mutual respect and shared responsibilities between girls and boys from pre-school level onward and develop, in particular, educational modules to ensure that boys have the skills necessary to take care of their own domestic needs and to share responsibility for their household and for the care of dependents;

(c) Develop training programs and materials for teachers and educators that raise awareness of their own role in the educational process, with a view to providing them with effective strategies for gender-sensitive teaching;

(d) Take actions to ensure that female teachers and professors have the same opportunities as and equal status with male teachers and professors, in view of the importance of having female teachers at all levels and in order to attract girls to school and retain them in school;

(e) Introduce and promote training in peaceful conflict resolution;

(f) Take positive measures to increase the proportion of women gaining access to educational policy- and decision-making, particularly women teachers at all levels of education and in academic disciplines that are traditionally male-dominated, such as the scientific and technological fields;

(g) Support and develop gender studies and research at all levels of education, especially at the postgraduate level of academic institutions, and apply them in the development of curricula, including university curricula, textbooks and teaching aids, and in teacher training;

(h) Develop leadership training and opportunities for all women to encourage them to take leadership roles both as students and as adults in civil society;

(i) Develop appropriate education and information programs with due respect for multilingualism, particularly in conjunction with the mass media, that make the public, particularly parents, aware of the importance of non-discriminatory education for children and the equal sharing of family responsibilities by girls and boys;

(j) Develop human rights education programs that incorporate the gender dimension at all levels of education, in particular by encouraging higher education institutions, especially in their graduate and postgraduate juridical, social and political science curricula, to include the study of the human rights of women as they appear in United Nations conventions;

(k) Remove legal, regulatory and social barriers, where appropriate, to sexual and reproductive health education within formal education programs regarding women's health issues;

(l) Encourage, with the guidance and support of their parents and in cooperation with educational staff and institutions, the elaboration of educational programs for girls and boys and the creation of integrated services in order to raise awareness of their responsibilities and to help them to assume those responsibilities, taking into account the importance of such education and services to personal development and self-esteem, as well as the urgent need to avoid unwanted pregnancy, the spread of sexually transmit-

ted diseases, especially HIV/AIDS, and such phenomena as sexual violence and abuse;

(m) Provide accessible recreational and sports facilities and establish and strengthen gender-sensitive programs for girls and women of all ages in education and community institutions and support the advancement of women in all areas of athletics and physical activity, including coaching, training and administration, and as participants at the national, regional and international levels;

(n) Recognize and support the right of indigenous women and girls to education and promote a multicultural approach to education that is responsive to the needs, aspirations and cultures of indigenous women, including by developing appropriate education programs, curricula and teaching aids, to the extent possible in the languages of indigenous people, and by providing for the participation of indigenous women in these processes;

(o) Acknowledge and respect the artistic, spiritual and cultural activities of indigenous women;

(p) Ensure that gender equality and cultural, religious and other diversity are respected in educational institutions;

(q) Promote education, training and relevant information programs for rural and farming women through the use of affordable and appropriate technologies and the mass media - for example, radio programs, cassettes and mobile units;

(r) Provide non-formal education, especially for rural women, in order to realize their potential with regard to health, micro-enterprise, agriculture and legal rights;

(s) Remove all barriers to access to formal education for pregnant adolescents and young mothers, and support the provision of child care and other support services where necessary.

STRATEGIC OBJECTIVE B.5.

> ❧ *Allocate sufficient resources for and monitor the implementation of educational reforms*

Actions to be taken

84. By Governments:

(a) Provide the required budgetary resources to the educational sector, with reallocation within the educational sector to ensure increased funds for basic education, as appropriate;

(b) Establish a mechanism at appropriate levels to monitor the implementation of educational reforms and measures in relevant ministries, and establish technical assistance programs, as appropriate, to address issues raised by the monitoring efforts.

85. By Governments and, as appropriate, private and public institutions, foundations, research institutes and non-governmental organizations:

(a) When necessary, mobilize additional funds from private and public institutions, foundations, research institutes and non-governmental organizations to enable girls and women, as well as boys and men on an equal basis, to complete their education, with particular emphasis on under-served populations;

(b) Provide funding for special programs, such as programs in mathematics, science and computer technology, to advance opportunities for all girls and women.

86. By multilateral development institutions, including the World Bank, regional development banks, bilateral donors and foundations:

(a) Consider increasing funding for the education and training needs of girls and women as a priority in development assistance programs;

(b) Consider working with recipient Governments to ensure that funding for women's education is maintained or increased in structural adjustment and economic recovery programs, including lending and stabilization programs.

87. By international and intergovernmental organizations, especially the United Nations Educational, Scientific and Cultural Organization, at the global level:

(a) Contribute to the evaluation of progress achieved, using educational indicators generated by national, regional and international bodies, and urge Governments, in implementing measures, to eliminate differences between women and men and boys and girls with regard to opportunities in education and training and the levels achieved in all fields, particularly in primary and literacy programs;

(b) Provide technical assistance upon request to developing countries to strengthen the capacity to monitor progress in closing the gap between women and men in education, training and research, and in levels of achievement in all fields, particularly basic education and the elimination of illiteracy;

(c) Conduct an international campaign promoting the right of women and girls to education;

(d) Allocate a substantial percentage of their resources to basic education for women and girls.

STRATEGIC OBJECTIVE B.6.

> ☙ *Promote life-long education and training for girls and women*

Actions to be taken

88. By Governments, educational institutions and communities:

(a) Ensure the availability of a broad range of educational and training programs that lead to ongoing acquisition by women and girls of the knowledge and skills required for living in, contributing to and benefiting from their communities and nations;

(b) Provide support for child care and other services to enable mothers to continue their schooling;

(c) Create flexible education, training and retraining programs for lifelong learning that facilitate transitions between women's activities at all stages of their lives.

Chapter IV. C

WOMEN AND HEALTH *

89. Women have the right to the enjoyment of the highest attainable standard of physical and mental health. The enjoyment of this right is vital to their life and well-being and their ability to participate in all areas of public and private life. Health is a state of complete physical, mental and social well-being and not merely the absence of disease or infirmity. Women's health involves their emotional, social and physical well-being and is determined by the social, political and economic context of their lives, as well as by biology. However, health and well-being elude the majority of women. A major barrier for women to the achievement of the highest attainable standard of health is inequality, both between men and women and among women in different geographical regions, social classes and indigenous and ethnic groups. In national and international forums, women have emphasized that to attain optimal health throughout the life cycle, equality, including the sharing of family responsibilities, development and peace are necessary conditions.

90. Women have different and unequal access to and use of basic health resources, including primary health services for the prevention and treatment of childhood diseases, malnutrition, anemia, diarrheal diseases, communicable diseases, malaria and other tropical diseases and tuberculosis, among others. Women also have different and unequal opportunities for the protection, promotion and maintenance of their health. In many developing countries, the lack of emergency obstetric services is also of particular concern. Health policies and programs often perpetuate gender stereotypes and fail to consider socio-economic disparities and other differences among women and may not fully take account of the lack of autonomy of women regarding their health. Women's health is also affected by

---

* The Holy See expressed a general reservation on this section. The reservation is to be interpreted in terms of the statement made by the representative of the Holy See at the 4th meeting of the Main Committee, on 14 September 1995 [see chap. V of the report, para. 11, not included in this edition, but available on the Internet at the following URL: http://www.undp.org/fwcw/daw1.htm]

gender bias in the health system and by the provision of inadequate and inappropriate medical services to women.

91. In many countries, especially developing countries, in particular the least developed countries, a decrease in public health spending and, in some cases, structural adjustment, contribute to the deterioration of public health systems. In addition, privatization of health-care systems without appropriate guarantees of universal access to affordable health care further reduces health-care availability. This situation not only directly affects the health of girls and women, but also places disproportionate responsibilities on women, whose multiple roles, including their roles within the family and the community, are often not acknowledged; hence they do not receive the necessary social, psychological and economic support.

92. Women's right to the enjoyment of the highest standard of health must be secured throughout the whole life cycle in equality with men. Women are affected by many of the same health conditions as men, but women experience them differently. The prevalence among women of poverty and economic dependence, their experience of violence, negative attitudes towards women and girls, racial and other forms of discrimination, the limited power many women have over their sexual and reproductive lives and lack of influence in decision-making are social realities which have an adverse impact on their health. Lack of food and inequitable distribution of food for girls and women in the household, inadequate access to safe water, sanitation facilities and fuel supplies, particularly in rural and poor urban areas, and deficient housing conditions, all overburden women and their families and have a negative effect on their health. Good health is essential to leading a productive and fulfilling life, and the right of all women to control all aspects of their health, in particular their own fertility, is basic to their empowerment.

93. Discrimination against girls, often resulting from son preference, in access to nutrition and health-care services endangers their current and future health and well-being. Conditions that force girls into early marriage, pregnancy and child-bearing and subject them to harmful practices, such as female genital mutilation, pose grave health risks. Adolescent girls need, but too often do not have, access to necessary health and nutrition services as they mature. Counseling and access to sexual and reproductive health information and services for adolescents are still inadequate or lacking completely, and a young woman's right to privacy, confidentiality, respect and informed consent is often not considered. Adolescent girls are both biologically and psycho-socially more vulnerable than boys to sexual abuse, violence and prostitution, and to the consequences of unprotected and premature sexual relations. The trend towards

early sexual experience, combined with a lack of information and services, increases the risk of unwanted and too early pregnancy, HIV infection and other sexually transmitted diseases, as well as unsafe abortions. Early child-bearing continues to be an impediment to improvements in the educational, economic and social status of women in all parts of the world. Overall, for young women early marriage and early motherhood can severely curtail educational and employment opportunities and are likely to have a long-term, adverse impact on the quality of their lives and the lives of their children. Young men are often not educated to respect women's self-determination and to share responsibility with women in matters of sexuality and reproduction.

94. Reproductive health is a state of complete physical, mental and social well-being and not merely the absence of disease or infirmity, in all matters relating to the reproductive system and to its functions and processes. Reproductive health therefore implies that people are able to have a satisfying and safe sex life and that they have the capability to reproduce and the freedom to decide if, when and how often to do so. Implicit in this last condition are the right of men and women to be informed and to have access to safe, effective, affordable and acceptable methods of family planning of their choice, as well as other methods of their choice for regulation of fertility which are not against the law, and the right of access to appropriate health-care services that will enable women to go safely through pregnancy and childbirth and provide couples with the best chance of having a healthy infant. In line with the above definition of reproductive health, reproductive health care is defined as the constellation of methods, techniques and services that contribute to reproductive health and well-being by preventing and solving reproductive health problems. It also includes sexual health, the purpose of which is the enhancement of life and personal relations, and not merely counseling and care related to reproduction and sexually transmitted diseases.

95. Bearing in mind the above definition, reproductive rights embrace certain human rights that are already recognized in national laws, international human rights documents and other consensus documents. These rights rest on the recognition of the basic right of all couples and individuals to decide freely and responsibly the number, spacing and timing of their children and to have the information and means to do so, and the right to attain the highest standard of sexual and reproductive health. It also includes their right to make decisions concerning reproduction free of discrimination, coercion and violence, as expressed in human rights documents. In the exercise of this right, they should take into account the needs of

their living and future children and their responsibilities towards the community. The promotion of the responsible exercise of these rights for all people should be the fundamental basis for government- and community-supported policies and programs in the area of reproductive health, including family planning. As part of their commitment, full attention should be given to the promotion of mutually respectful and equitable gender relations and particularly to meeting the educational and service needs of adolescents to enable them to deal in a positive and responsible way with their sexuality. Reproductive health eludes many of the world's people because of such factors as: inadequate levels of knowledge about human sexuality and inappropriate or poor-quality reproductive health information and services; the prevalence of high-risk sexual behavior; discriminatory social practices; negative attitudes towards women and girls; and the limited power many women and girls have over their sexual and reproductive lives. Adolescents are particularly vulnerable because of their lack of information and access to relevant services in most countries. Older women and men have distinct reproductive and sexual health issues which are often inadequately addressed.

96. The human rights of women include their right to have control over and decide freely and responsibly on matters related to their sexuality, including sexual and reproductive health, free of coercion, discrimination and violence. Equal relationships between women and men in matters of sexual relations and reproduction, including full respect for the integrity of the person, require mutual respect, consent and shared responsibility for sexual behavior and its consequences.

97. Further, women are subject to particular health risks due to inadequate responsiveness and lack of services to meet health needs related to sexuality and reproduction. Complications related to pregnancy and childbirth are among the leading causes of mortality and morbidity of women of reproductive age in many parts of the developing world. Similar problems exist to a certain degree in some countries with economies in transition. Unsafe abortions threaten the lives of a large number of women, representing a grave public health problem as it is primarily the poorest and youngest who take the highest risk. Most of these deaths, health problems and injuries are preventable through improved access to adequate health-care services, including safe and effective family planning methods and emergency obstetric care, recognizing the right of women and men to be informed and to have access to safe, effective, affordable and acceptable methods of family planning of their choice, as well as other methods of their choice for regulation of fertility which are

not against the law, and the right of access to appropriate health-care services that will enable women to go safely through pregnancy and childbirth and provide couples with the best chance of having a healthy infant. These problems and means should be addressed on the basis of the report of the International Conference on Population and Development, with particular reference to relevant paragraphs of the Program of Action of the Conference. 14/ In most countries, the neglect of women's reproductive rights severely limits their opportunities in public and private life, including opportunities for education and economic and political empowerment. The ability of women to control their own fertility forms an important basis for the enjoyment of other rights. Shared responsibility between women and men in matters related to sexual and reproductive behavior is also essential to improving women's health.

98. HIV/AIDS and other sexually transmitted diseases, the transmission of which is sometimes a consequence of sexual violence, are having a devastating effect on women's health, particularly the health of adolescent girls and young women. They often do not have the power to insist on safe and responsible sex practices and have little access to information and services for prevention and treatment. Women, who represent half of all adults newly infected with HIV/AIDS and other sexually transmitted diseases, have emphasized that social vulnerability and the unequal power relationships between women and men are obstacles to safe sex, in their efforts to control the spread of sexually transmitted diseases. The consequences of HIV/AIDS reach beyond women's health to their role as mothers and caregivers and their contribution to the economic support of their families. The social, developmental and health consequences of HIV/AIDS and other sexually transmitted diseases need to be seen from a gender perspective.

99. Sexual and gender-based violence, including physical and psychological abuse, trafficking in women and girls, and other forms of abuse and sexual exploitation place girls and women at high risk of physical and mental trauma, disease and unwanted pregnancy. Such situations often deter women from using health and other services.

100. Mental disorders related to marginalization, powerlessness and poverty, along with overwork and stress and the growing incidence of domestic violence as well as substance abuse, are among other health issues of growing concern to women. Women throughout the world, especially young women, are increasing their use of tobacco with serious effects on their health and that of their children. Occupational health issues are also growing in importance, as a large number of women work in low-paid jobs in either the formal or the

informal labor market under tedious and unhealthy conditions, and the number is rising. Cancers of the breast and cervix and other cancers of the reproductive system, as well as infertility affect growing numbers of women and may be preventable, or curable, if detected early.

101. With the increase in life expectancy and the growing number of older women, their health concerns require particular attention. The long-term health prospects of women are influenced by changes at menopause, which, in combination with life-long conditions and other factors, such as poor nutrition and lack of physical activity, may increase the risk of cardiovascular disease and osteoporosis. Other diseases of aging and the interrelationships of aging and disability among women also need particular attention.

102. Women, like men, particularly in rural areas and poor urban areas, are increasingly exposed to environmental health hazards owing to environmental catastrophes and degradation. Women have a different susceptibility to various environmental hazards, contaminants and substances and they suffer different consequences from exposure to them.

103. The quality of women's health care is often deficient in various ways, depending on local circumstances. Women are frequently not treated with respect, nor are they guaranteed privacy and confidentiality, nor do they always receive full information about the options and services available. Furthermore, in some countries, over-medicating of women's life events is common, leading to unnecessary surgical intervention and inappropriate medication.

104. Statistical data on health are often not systematically collected, disaggregated and analyzed by age, sex and socio-economic status and by established demographic criteria used to serve the interests and solve the problems of subgroups, with particular emphasis on the vulnerable and marginalized and other relevant variables. Recent and reliable data on the mortality and morbidity of women and conditions and diseases particularly affecting women are not available in many countries. Relatively little is known about how social and economic factors affect the health of girls and women of all ages, about the provision of health services to girls and women and the patterns of their use of such services, and about the value of disease prevention and health promotion programs for women. Subjects of importance to women's health have not been adequately researched and women's health research often lacks funding. Medical research, on heart disease, for example, and epidemiological studies in many countries are often based solely on men; they are not gender specific. Clinical trials involving women to establish basic information about dosage, side-effects and effectiveness of

drugs, including contraceptives, are noticeably absent and do not always conform to ethical standards for research and testing. Many drug therapy protocols and other medical treatments and interventions administered to women are based on research on men without any investigation and adjustment for gender differences.

105. In addressing inequalities in health status and unequal access to and inadequate health-care services between women and men, Governments and other actors should promote an active and visible policy of mainstreaming a gender perspective in all policies and programs, so that, before decisions are taken, an analysis is made of the effects for women and men, respectively.

STRATEGIC OBJECTIVE C. 1.

> ❧ *Increase women's access throughout the life cycle to appropriate, affordable and quality health care, information and related services*

Actions to be taken

106. By Governments, in collaboration with non-governmental organizations and employers' and workers' organizations and with the support of international institutions:

(a) Support and implement the commitments made in the Program of Action of the International Conference on Population and Development, as established in the report of that Conference and the Copenhagen Declaration on Social Development and Program of Action of the World Summit for Social Development 15/ and the obligations of States parties under the Convention on the Elimination of All Forms of Discrimination against Women and other relevant international agreements, to meet the health needs of girls and women of all ages;

(b) Reaffirm the right to the enjoyment of the highest attainable standards of physical and mental health, protect and promote the attainment of this right for women and girls and incorporate it in national legislation, for example; review existing legislation, including health legislation, as well as policies, where necessary, to reflect a commitment to women's health and to ensure that they meet the changing roles and responsibilities of women wherever they reside;

(c) Design and implement, in cooperation with women and community-based organizations, gender-sensitive health programs, including decentralized health services, that address the needs of women throughout their lives and take into account their multiple roles and responsibilities, the demands on their time, the special needs of rural women and women with disabilities and the diversity of women's needs arising from age and socio-economic and cultural differences, among others; include women, especially local and indigenous women, in the identification and planning of health-care priorities and programs; remove all barriers to women's health services and provide a broad range of health-care services;

(d) Allow women access to social security systems in equality with men throughout the whole life cycle;

(e) Provide more accessible, available and affordable primary health-care services of high quality, including sexual and reproductive health care, which includes family planning information and services, and giving particular attention to maternal and emergency obstetric care, as agreed to in the Program of Action of the International Conference on Population and Development;

(f) Redesign health information, services and training for health workers so that they are gender-sensitive and reflect the user's perspectives with regard to interpersonal and communications skills and the user's right to privacy and confidentiality; these services, information and training should be based on a holistic approach;

(g) Ensure that all health services and workers conform to human rights and to ethical, professional and gender-sensitive standards in the delivery of women's health services aimed at ensuring responsible, voluntary and informed consent; encourage the development, implementation and dissemination of codes of ethics guided by existing international codes of medical ethics as well as ethical principles that govern other health professionals;

(h) Take all appropriate measures to eliminate harmful, medically unnecessary or coercive medical interventions, as well as inappropriate medication and over-medication of women, and ensure that all women are fully informed of their options, including likely benefits and potential side-effects, by properly trained personnel;

(i) Strengthen and reorient health services, particularly primary health care, in order to ensure universal access to quality health services for women and girls; reduce ill health and maternal morbidity and achieve world wide the agreed-upon goal of reducing maternal mortality by at least 50 per cent of the 1990 levels by the year 2000 and a further one half by the year 2015; ensure that the necessary services are available at each level of the health system and make reproductive health care accessible, through the primary health-care system, to all individuals of appropriate ages as soon as possible and no later than the year 2015;

(j) Recognize and deal with the health impact of unsafe abortion as a major public health concern, as agreed in paragraph 8.25 of the Program of Action of the International Conference on Population and Development; 14/

(k) In the light of paragraph 8.25 of the Program of Action of the International Conference on Population and Development, which states: "In no case should abortion be promoted as a method of family planning. All Governments and relevant intergovernmental and non-governmental organizations are urged to strengthen their commitment to women's health, to deal with the health impact of unsafe abortion 16/ as a major public health concern and to reduce the recourse to abortion through expanded and improved family-planning services. Prevention of unwanted pregnancies must always be given the highest priority and every attempt should be made to eliminate the need for abortion. Women who have unwanted pregnancies should have ready access to reliable information and compassionate counseling. Any measures or changes related to abortion within the health system can only be determined at the national or local level according to the national legislative process. In circumstances where abortion is not against the law, such abortion should be safe. In all cases, women should have access to quality services for the management of complications arising from abortion. Post-abortion counseling, education and family-planning services should be offered promptly, which will also help to avoid repeat abortions", consider reviewing laws containing punitive measures against women who have undergone illegal abortions;

(l) Give particular attention to the needs of girls, especially the promotion of healthy behavior, including physical activities; take specific measures for closing the gender gaps in morbidity and mortality where girls are disadvantaged, while achieving internationally approved goals for the reduction of infant and child mortality - specifically, by the year 2000, the reduction of mortality rates of infants and children under five years of age by one third of the 1990 level, or 50 to 70 per 1,000 live births, whichever is less; by the year 2015 an infant mortality rate below 35 per 1,000 live births and an under-five mortality rate below 45 per 1,000;

(m) Ensure that girls have continuing access to necessary health and nutrition information and services as they mature, to facilitate a healthful transition from childhood to adulthood;

(n) Develop information, programs and services to assist women to understand and adapt to changes associated with aging and to address and treat the health needs of older women, paying particular attention to those who are physically or psychologically dependent;

(o) Ensure that girls and women of all ages with any form of disability receive supportive services;

(p) Formulate special policies, design programs and enact the legislation necessary to alleviate and eliminate environmental and occupational health hazards associated with work in the home, in the workplace and elsewhere with attention to pregnant and lactating women;

(q) Integrate mental health services into primary health-care systems or other appropriate levels, develop supportive programs and train primary health workers to recognize and care for girls and women of all ages who have experienced any form of violence especially domestic violence, sexual abuse or other abuse resulting from armed and non-armed conflict;

(r) Promote public information on the benefits of breast-feeding; examine ways and means of implementing fully the WHO/UNICEF International Code of Marketing of Breast-milk Substitutes, and enable mothers to breastfeed their infants by providing legal, economic, practical and emotional support;

(s) Establish mechanisms to support and involve non-governmental organizations, particularly women's organizations, professional groups and other bodies working to improve the health of girls and women, in government policy-making, program design, as appropriate, and implementation within the health sector and related sectors at all levels;

(t) Support non-governmental organizations working on women's health and help develop networks aimed at improving coordination and collaboration between all sectors that affect health;

(u) Rationalize drug procurement and ensure a reliable, continuous supply of high-quality pharmaceutical, contraceptive and other supplies and equipment, using the WHO Model List of Essential Drugs as a guide, and ensure the safety of drugs and devices through national regulatory drug approval processes;

(v) Provide improved access to appropriate treatment and rehabilitation services for women substance abusers and their families;

(w) Promote and ensure household and national food security, as appropriate, and implement programs aimed at improving the nutritional status of all girls and women by implementing the commitments made in the Plan of Action on Nutrition of the International Conference on Nutrition, 17/ including a reduction world wide of severe and moderate malnutrition among children under the age of five by one half of 1990 levels by the year 2000, giving special attention to the gender gap in nutrition, and a reduction in iron deficiency anemia in girls and women by one third of the 1990 levels by the year 2000;

(x) Ensure the availability of and universal access to safe drinking water and sanitation and put in place effective public distribution systems as soon as possible;

(y) Ensure full and equal access to health-care infrastructure and services for indigenous women.

STRATEGIC OBJECTIVE C.2.

❧ *Strengthen preventive programs that promote women's health*

Actions to be taken

107. By Governments, in cooperation with non-governmental organizations, the mass media, the private sector and relevant international organizations, including United Nations bodies, as appropriate:

(a) Give priority to both formal and informal educational programs that support and enable women to develop self-esteem, acquire knowledge, make decisions on and take responsibility for their own health, achieve mutual respect in matters concerning sexuality and fertility and educate men regarding the importance of women's health and well-being, placing special focus on programs for both men and women that emphasize the elimination of harmful attitudes and practices, including female genital mutilation, son preference(which results in female infanticide and prenatal sex selection), early marriage, including child marriage, violence against women, sexual exploitation, sexual abuse, which at times is conducive to infection with HIV/AIDS and other sexually transmitted diseases, drug abuse, discrimination against girls and women in food allocation and other harmful attitudes and practices related to the life, health and well-being of women, and recognizing that some of these practices can be violations of human rights and ethical medical principles;

(b) Pursue social, human development, education and employment policies to eliminate poverty among women in order to reduce their susceptibility to ill health and to improve their health;

(c) Encourage men to share equally in child care and household work and to provide their share of financial support for their families, even if they do not live with them;

(d) Reinforce laws, reform institutions and promote norms and practices that eliminate discrimination against women and encourage both women and men to take responsibility for their sexual and reproductive behavior; ensure full respect for the integrity of the person, take action to ensure the conditions necessary for women to exercise their reproductive rights and eliminate coercive laws and practices;

(e) Prepare and disseminate accessible information, through public health campaigns, the media, reliable counseling and the education system, designed to ensure that women and men, particularly young people, can acquire knowledge about their health, especially information on sexuality and reproduction, taking into account the rights of the child to access to information, privacy, confidentiality, respect and informed consent, as well as the responsibilities, rights and duties of parents and legal guardians to provide, in a manner consistent with the evolving capacities of the child, appropriate direction and guidance in the exercise by the child of the rights recognized in the Convention on the Rights of the Child, and in conformity with the Convention on the Elimination of All Forms of Discrimination against Women; ensure that in all actions concerning children, the best interests of the child are a primary consideration;

(f) Create and support programs in the educational system, in the workplace and in the community to make opportunities to participate in sport, physical activity and recreation available to girls and women of all ages on the same basis as they are made available to men and boys;

(g) Recognize the specific needs of adolescents and implement specific appropriate programs, such as education and information on sexual and reproductive health issues and on sexually transmitted diseases, including HIV/AIDS, taking into account the rights of the child and the responsibilities, rights and duties of parents as stated in paragraph 107*(e)* above;

(h) Develop policies that reduce the disproportionate and increasing burden on women who have multiple roles within the family and the community by providing them with adequate support and programs from health and social services;

(i) Adopt regulations to ensure that the working conditions, including remuneration and promotion of women at all levels of the health system, are non-discriminatory and meet fair and professional standards to enable them to work effectively;

(j) Ensure that health and nutritional information and training form an integral part of all adult literacy programs and school curricula from the primary level;

(k) Develop and undertake media campaigns and information and educational programs that inform women and girls of the health and related risks of substance abuse and addiction and pursue strategies and programs that discourage substance abuse and addiction and promote rehabilitation and recovery;

(l) Devise and implement comprehensive and coherent programs for the prevention, diagnosis and treatment of osteoporosis, a condition that predominantly affects women;

(m) Establish and/or strengthen programs and services, including media campaigns, that address the prevention, early detection and treatment of breast, cervical and other cancers of the reproductive system;

(n) Reduce environmental hazards that pose a growing threat to health, especially in poor regions and communities; apply a precautionary approach, as agreed to in the Rio Declaration on Environment and Development, adopted by the United Nations Conference on Environment and Development, 18/ and include reporting on women's health risks related to the environment in monitoring the implementation of Agenda 21; 19/

(o) Create awareness among women, health professionals, policy makers and the general public about the serious but preventable health hazards stemming from tobacco consumption and the need for regulatory and education measures to reduce smoking as important health promotion and disease prevention activities;

(p) Ensure that medical school curricula and other health-care training include gender-sensitive, comprehensive and mandatory courses on women's health;

(q) Adopt specific preventive measures to protect women, youth and children from any abuse - sexual abuse, exploitation, trafficking and violence, for example - including the formulation and enforcement of laws, and provide legal protection and medical and other assistance.

STRATEGIC OBJECTIVE C. 3.

> ❧ *Undertake gender-sensitive initiatives that address sexually transmitted diseases, HIV/AIDS, and sexual and reproductive health issues*

Actions to be taken

108. By Governments, international bodies including relevant United Nations organizations, bilateral and multilateral donors and non governmental organizations:

(a) Ensure the involvement of women, especially those infected with HIV/AIDS or other sexually transmitted diseases or affected by the HIV/AIDS pandemic, in all decision-making relating to the development, implementation, monitoring and evaluation of policies and programs on HIV/AIDS and other sexually transmitted diseases;

(b) Review and amend laws and combat practices, as appropriate, that may contribute to women's susceptibility to HIV infection and other sexually transmitted diseases, including enacting legislation against those socio-cultural practices that contribute to it, and implement legislation, policies and practices to protect women, adolescents and young girls from discrimination related to HIV/AIDS;

(c) Encourage all sectors of society, including the public sector, as well as international organizations, to develop compassionate and supportive, non-discriminatory HIV/AIDS-related policies and practices that protect the rights of infected individuals;

(d) Recognize the extent of the HIV/AIDS pandemic in their countries, taking particularly into account its impact on women, with a view to ensuring that infected women do not suffer stigmatization and discrimination, including during travel;

(e) Develop gender-sensitive multisectoral programs and strategies to end social subordination of women and girls and to ensure their social and economic empowerment and equality; facilitate promotion of programs to educate and enable men to assume their responsibilities to prevent HIV/AIDS and other sexually transmitted diseases;

(f) Facilitate the development of community strategies that will protect women of all ages from HIV and other sexually transmitted diseases; provide care and support to infected girls, women and their families and mobilize all parts of the community in response to the HIV/AIDS pandemic to

exert pressure on all responsible authorities to respond in a timely, effective, sustainable and gender-sensitive manner;

(g) Support and strengthen national capacity to create and improve gender-sensitive policies and programs on HIV/AIDS and other sexually transmitted diseases, including the provision of resources and facilities to women who find themselves the principal caregivers or economic support for those infected with HIV/AIDS or affected by the pandemic, and the survivors, particularly children and older persons;

(h) Provide workshops and specialized education and training to parents, decision makers and opinion leaders at all levels of the community, including religious and traditional authorities, on prevention of HIV/AIDS and other sexually transmitted diseases and on their repercussions on both women and men of all ages;

(i) Give all women and health workers all relevant information and education about sexually transmitted diseases including HIV/AIDS and pregnancy and the implications for the baby, including breast-feeding;

(j) Assist women and their formal and informal organizations to establish and expand effective peer education and outreach programs and to participate in the design, implementation and monitoring of these programs;

(k) Give full attention to the promotion of mutually respectful and equitable gender relations and, in particular, to meeting the educational and service needs of adolescents to enable them to deal in a positive and responsible way with their sexuality;

(l) Design specific programs for men of all ages and male adolescents, recognizing the parental roles referred to in paragraph 107*(e)* above, aimed at providing complete and accurate information on safe and responsible sexual and reproductive behavior, including voluntary, appropriate and effective male methods for the prevention of HIV/AIDS and other sexually transmitted diseases through, *inter alia*, abstinence and condom use;

(m) Ensure the provision, through the primary health-care system, of universal access of couples and individuals to appropriate and affordable preventive services with respect to sexually transmitted diseases, including HIV/AIDS, and expand the provision of counseling and voluntary and confidential diagnostic and treatment services for women; ensure that high-quality condoms as well as drugs for the treatment of sexually transmitted diseases are, where possible, supplied and distributed to health services;

(n) Support programs which acknowledge that the higher risk among women of contracting HIV is linked to high-risk behavior, including intravenous substance use and substance-influenced unprotected and irresponsible sexual behavior, and take appropriate preventive measures;

(o) Support and expedite action-oriented research on affordable methods, controlled by women, to prevent HIV and other sexually transmitted diseases, on strategies empowering women to protect themselves from sexually

transmitted diseases, including HIV/AIDS, and on methods of care, support and treatment of women, ensuring their involvement in all aspects of such research;

(p) Support and initiate research which addresses women's needs and situations, including research on HIV infection and other sexually transmitted diseases in women, on women-controlled methods of protection, such as non-spermicidal microbicides, and on male and female risk-taking attitudes and practices.

STRATEGIC OBJECTIVE C. 4.

> ❧ *Promote research and disseminate information on women's health*

Actions to be taken

109. By Governments, the United Nations system, health professions, research institutions, non-governmental organizations, donors, pharmaceutical industries and the mass media, as appropriate:

(a) Train researchers and introduce systems that allow for the use of data collected, analyzed and disaggregated by, among other factors, sex and age, other established demographic criteria and socio-economic variables, in policy-making, as appropriate, planning, monitoring and evaluation;

(b) Promote gender-sensitive and women-centered health research, treatment and technology and link traditional and indigenous knowledge with modern medicine, making information available to women to enable them to make informed and responsible decisions;

(c) Increase the number of women in leadership positions in the health professions, including researchers and scientists, to achieve equality at the earliest possible date;

(d) Increase financial and other support from all sources for preventive, appropriate biomedical, behavioral, epidemiological and health service research on women's health issues and for research on the social, economic and political causes of women's health problems, and their consequences, including the impact of gender and age inequalities, especially with respect to chronic and non-communicable diseases, particularly cardiovascular diseases and conditions, cancers, reproductive tract infections and injuries, HIV/AIDS and other sexually transmitted diseases, domestic violence, occupational health, disabilities, environmentally related health problems, tropical diseases and health aspects of aging;

(e) Inform women about the factors which increase the risks of developing cancers and infections of the reproductive tract, so that they can make informed decisions about their health;

(f) Support and fund social, economic, political and cultural research on how gender-based inequalities affect women's health, including etiology, epidemiology, provision and utilization of services and eventual outcome of treatment;

(g) Support health service systems and operations research to strengthen access and improve the quality of service delivery, to ensure appropriate support for women as health-care providers and to examine patterns with respect to the provision of health services to women and use of such services by women;

(h) Provide financial and institutional support for research on safe, effective, affordable and acceptable methods and technologies for the reproductive and sexual health of women and men, including more safe, effective, affordable and acceptable methods for the regulation of fertility, including natural family planning for both sexes, methods to protect against HIV/AIDS and other sexually transmitted diseases and simple and inexpensive methods of diagnosing such diseases, among others; this research needs to be guided at all stages by users and from the perspective of gender, particularly the perspective of women, and should be carried out in strict conformity with internationally accepted legal, ethical, medical and scientific standards for biomedical research;

(i) Since unsafe abortion 16/ is a major threat to the health and life of women, research to understand and better address the determinants and consequences of induced abortion, including its effects on subsequent fertility, reproductive and mental health and contraceptive practice, should be promoted, as well as research on treatment of complications of abortions and post-abortion care;

(j) Acknowledge and encourage beneficial traditional health care, especially that practiced by indigenous women, with a view to preserving and incorporating the value of traditional health care in the provision of health services, and support research directed towards achieving this aim;

(k) Develop mechanisms to evaluate and disseminate available data and research findings to researchers, policy makers, health professionals and women's groups, among others;

(l) Monitor human genome and related genetic research from the perspective of women's health and disseminate information and results of studies conducted in accordance with accepted ethical standards.

STRATEGIC OBJECTIVE C.5.

> ❧ *Increase resources and monitor follow-up for women's health*

Actions to be taken

110. By Governments at all levels and, where appropriate, in cooperation with non-governmental organizations, especially women's and youth organizations:

(a) Increase budgetary allocations for primary health care and social services, with adequate support for secondary and tertiary levels, and give special attention to the reproductive and sexual health of girls and women and give priority to health programs in rural and poor urban areas;

(b) Develop innovative approaches to funding health services through promoting community participation and local financing; increase, where necessary, budgetary allocations for community health centers and community-based programs and services that address women's specific health needs;

(c) Develop local health services, promoting the incorporation of gender sensitive community-based participation and self-care and specially designed preventive health programs;

(d) Develop goals and time-frames, where appropriate, for improving women's health and for planning, implementing, monitoring and evaluating programs, based on gender-impact assessments using qualitative and quantitative data disaggregated by sex, age, other established demographic criteria and socio-economic variables;

(e) Establish, as appropriate, ministerial and interministerial mechanisms for monitoring the implementation of women's health policy and program reforms and establish, as appropriate, high-level focal points in national planning authorities responsible for monitoring to ensure that women's health concerns are mainstreamed in all relevant government agencies and programs.

111. By Governments, the United Nations and its specialized agencies, international financial institutions, bilateral donors and the private sector, as appropriate:

(a) Formulate policies favorable to investment in women's health and, where appropriate, increase allocations for such investment;

(b) Provide appropriate material, financial and logistical assistance to youth non-governmental organizations in order to strengthen them to address youth concerns in the area of health, including sexual and reproductive health;

(c) Give higher priority to women's health and develop mechanisms for coordinating and implementing the health objectives of the PLATFORM FOR ACTION and relevant international agreements to ensure progress.

Chapter IV. D

VIOLENCE AGAINST WOMEN

112. Violence against women is an obstacle to the achievement of the objectives of equality, development and peace. Violence against women both violates and impairs or nullifies the enjoyment by women of their human rights and fundamental freedoms. The long-standing failure to protect and promote those rights and freedoms in the case of violence against women is a matter of concern to all States and should be addressed. Knowledge about its causes and consequences, as well as its incidence and measures to combat it, have been greatly expanded since the Nairobi Conference. In all societies, to a greater or lesser degree, women and girls are subjected to physical, sexual and psychological abuse that cuts across lines of income, class and culture. The low social and economic status of women can be both a cause and a consequence of violence against women.

113. The term "violence against women" means any act of gender-based violence that results in, or is likely to result in, physical, sexual or psychological harm or suffering to women, including threats of such acts, coercion or arbitrary deprivation of liberty, whether occurring in public or private life. Accordingly, violence against women encompasses but is not limited to the following:

(a) Physical, sexual and psychological violence occurring in the family, including battering, sexual abuse of female children in the household, dowry-related violence, marital rape, female genital mutilation and other traditional practices harmful to women, non-spousal violence and violence related to exploitation;

(b) Physical, sexual and psychological violence occurring within the general community, including rape, sexual abuse, sexual harassment and intimidation at work, in educational institutions and elsewhere, trafficking in women and forced prostitution;

(c) Physical, sexual and psychological violence perpetrated or condoned by the State, wherever it occurs.

114. Other acts of violence against women include violation of the human rights of women in situations of armed conflict, in particular murder, systematic rape, sexual slavery and forced pregnancy.

115. Acts of violence against women also include forced sterilization and forced abortion, coercive/forced use of contraceptives, female infanticide and prenatal sex selection.

116. Some groups of women, such as women belonging to minority groups, indigenous women, refugee women, women migrants, including women migrant workers, women in poverty living in rural or remote communities, destitute women, women in institutions or in detention, female children, women with disabilities, elderly women, displaced women, repatriated women, women living in poverty and women in situations of armed conflict, foreign occupation, wars of aggression, civil wars, terrorism, including hostage taking, are also particularly vulnerable to violence.

117. Acts or threats of violence, whether occurring within the home or in the community, or perpetrated or condoned by the State, instill fear and insecurity in women's lives and are obstacles to the achievement of equality and for development and peace. The fear of violence, including harassment, is a permanent constraint on the mobility of women and limits their access to resources and basic activities. High social, health and economic costs to the individual and society are associated with violence against women. Violence against women is one of the crucial social mechanisms by which women are forced into a subordinate position compared with men. In many cases, violence against women and girls occurs in the family or within the home, where violence is often tolerated. The neglect, physical and sexual abuse, and rape of girl children and women by family members and other members of the household, as well as incidences of spousal and non-spousal abuse, often go unreported and are thus difficult to detect. Even when such violence is reported, there is often a failure to protect victims or punish perpetrators.

118. Violence against women is a manifestation of the historically unequal power relations between men and women, which have led to domination over and discrimination against women by men and to the prevention of women's full advancement. Violence against women throughout the life cycle derives essentially from cultural patterns, in particular the harmful effects of certain traditional or customary practices and all acts of extremism linked to race, sex, language or religion that perpetuate the lower status accorded to women in the family, the workplace, the community and society. Violence against women is exacerbated by social pressures, notably the shame of denouncing certain acts that have been perpetrated against women; women's lack of access to legal information, aid or protection; the lack of laws that effectively prohibit violence against women; failure to reform existing laws; inadequate efforts on the

part of public authorities to promote awareness of and enforce existing laws; and the absence of educational and other means to address the causes and consequences of violence. Images in the media of violence against women, in particular those that depict rape or sexual slavery as well as the use of women and girls as sex objects, including pornography, are factors contributing to the continued prevalence of such violence, adversely influencing the community at large, in particular children and young people.

119. Developing a holistic and multidisciplinary approach to the challenging task of promoting families, communities and States that are free of violence against women is necessary and achievable. Equality, partnership between women and men and respect for human dignity must permeate all stages of the socialization process. Educational systems should promote self-respect, mutual respect, and cooperation between women and men.

120. The absence of adequate gender-disaggregated data and statistics on the incidence of violence makes the elaboration of programs and monitoring of changes difficult. Lack of or inadequate documentation and research on domestic violence, sexual harassment and violence against women and girls in private and in public, including the workplace, impede efforts to design specific intervention strategies. Experience in a number of countries shows that women and men can be mobilized to overcome violence in all its forms and that effective public measures can be taken to address both the causes and the consequences of violence. Men's groups mobilizing against gender violence are necessary allies for change.

121. Women may be vulnerable to violence perpetrated by persons in positions of authority in both conflict and non-conflict situations. Training of all officials in humanitarian and human rights law and the punishment of perpetrators of violent acts against women would help to ensure that such violence does not take place at the hands of public officials in whom women should be able to place trust, including police and prison officials and security forces.

122. The effective suppression of trafficking in women and girls for the sex trade is a matter of pressing international concern. Implementation of the 1949 Convention for the Suppression of the Traffic in Persons and of the Exploitation of the Prostitution of Others,[20] as well as other relevant instruments, needs to be reviewed and strengthened. The use of women in international prostitution and trafficking networks has become a major focus of international organized crime. The Special Rapporteur of the Commission on Human Rights on violence against women, who has explored these acts as an additional cause of the violation of the human rights and fundamental freedoms of women and girls, is invited to address, within

her mandate and as a matter of urgency, the issue of international trafficking for the purposes of the sex trade, as well as the issues of forced prostitution, rape, sexual abuse and sex tourism. Women and girls who are victims of this international trade are at an increased risk of further violence, as well as unwanted pregnancy and sexually transmitted infection, including infection with HIV/AIDS.

123. In addressing violence against women, Governments and other actors should promote an active and visible policy of mainstreaming a gender perspective in all policies and programs so that before decisions are taken an analysis may be made of their effects on women and men, respectively.

STRATEGIC OBJECTIVE D. 1.

> Take integrated measures to prevent and eliminate violence against women

Actions to be taken

124. By Governments:

(a) Condemn violence against women and refrain from invoking any custom, tradition or religious consideration to avoid their obligations with respect to its elimination as set out in the Declaration on the Elimination of Violence against Women;

(b) Refrain from engaging in violence against women and exercise due diligence to prevent, investigate and, in accordance with national legislation, punish acts of violence against women, whether those acts are perpetrated by the State or by private persons;

(c) Enact and/or reinforce penal, civil, labor and administrative sanctions in domestic legislation to punish and redress the wrongs done to women and girls who are subjected to any form of violence, whether in the home, the workplace, the community or society;

(d) Adopt and/or implement and periodically review and analyze legislation to ensure its effectiveness in eliminating violence against women, emphasizing the prevention of violence and the prosecution of offenders; take measures to ensure the protection of women subjected to violence, access to just and effective remedies, including compensation and indemnification and healing of victims, and rehabilitation of perpetrators;

(e) Work actively to ratify and/or implement international human rights norms and instruments as they relate to violence against women, including those contained in the Universal Declaration of Human Rights,[21] the International Covenant on Civil and Political Rights,[13] the International Covenant on Economic, Social and Cultural Rights,[13] and the Convention against Torture and Other Cruel, Inhuman or Degrading Treatment or Punishment;[22]

(f) Implement the Convention on the Elimination of All Forms of Discrimination against Women, taking into account general recommendation 19, adopted by the Committee on the Elimination of Discrimination against Women at its eleventh session;[23]

(g) Promote an active and visible policy of mainstreaming a gender perspective in all policies and programs related to violence against women; actively encourage, support and implement measures and programs aimed at increasing the knowledge and understanding of the causes, consequences and mechanisms of violence against women among those responsible for implementing these policies, such as law enforcement officers, police personnel and judicial, medical and social workers, as well as those who deal with minority, migration and refugee issues, and develop strategies to ensure that the revictimization of women victims of violence does not occur because of gender-insensitive laws or judicial or enforcement practices;

(h) Provide women who are subjected to violence with access to the mechanisms of justice and, as provided for by national legislation, to just and effective remedies for the harm they have suffered and inform women of their rights in seeking redress through such mechanisms;

(i) Enact and enforce legislation against the perpetrators of practices and acts of violence against women, such as female genital mutilation, female infanticide, prenatal sex selection and dowry-related violence, and give vigorous support to the efforts of non-governmental and community organizations to eliminate such practices;

(j) Formulate and implement, at all appropriate levels, plans of action to eliminate violence against women;

(k) Adopt all appropriate measures, especially in the field of education, to modify the social and cultural patterns of conduct of men and women, and to eliminate prejudices, customary practices and all other practices based on the idea of the inferiority or superiority of either of the sexes and on stereotyped roles for men and women;

(l) Create or strengthen institutional mechanisms so that women and girls can report acts of violence against them in a safe and confidential environment, free from the fear of penalties or retaliation, and file charges;

(m) Ensure that women with disabilities have access to information and services in the field of violence against women;

(n) Create, improve or develop as appropriate, and fund the training programs for judicial, legal, medical, social, educational and police and immigrant personnel, in order to avoid the abuse of power leading to violence against women and sensitize such personnel to the nature of gender-based acts and threats of violence so that fair treatment of female victims can be assured;

(o) Adopt laws, where necessary, and reinforce existing laws that punish police, security forces or any other agents of the State who engage in acts of violence against women in the course of the performance of their duties; review existing legislation and take effective measures against the perpetrators of such violence;

(p) Allocate adequate resources within the government budget and mobilize community resources for activities related to the elimination of violence against women, including resources for the implementation of plans of action at all appropriate levels;

(q) Include in reports submitted in accordance with the provisions of relevant United Nations human rights instruments, information pertaining to violence against women and measures taken to implement the Declaration on the Elimination of Violence against Women;

(r) Cooperate with and assist the Special Rapporteur of the Commission on Human Rights on violence against women in the performance of her mandate and furnish all information requested; cooperate also with other competent mechanisms, such as the Special Rapporteur of the Commission on Human Rights on torture and the Special Rapporteur of the Commission on Human Rights on summary, extra-judiciary and arbitrary executions, in relation to violence against women;

(s) Recommend that the Commission on Human Rights renew the mandate of the Special Rapporteur on violence against women when her term ends in 1997 and, if warranted, to update and strengthen it.

125. By Governments, including local governments, community organizations, non-governmental organizations, educational institutions, the public and private sectors, particularly enterprises, and the mass media, as appropriate:

(a) Provide well-funded shelters and relief support for girls and women subjected to violence, as well as medical, psychological and other counseling services and free or low-cost legal aid, where it is needed, as well as appropriate assistance to enable them to find a means of subsistence;

(b) Establish linguistically and culturally accessible services for migrant women and girls, including women migrant workers, who are victims of gender-based violence;

(c) Recognize the vulnerability to violence and other forms of abuse of women migrants, including women migrant workers, whose legal status in the host country depends on employers who may exploit their situation;

(d) Support initiatives of women's organizations and non-governmental organizations all over the world to raise awareness on the issue of violence against women and to contribute to its elimination;

(e) Organize, support and fund community-based education and training campaigns to raise awareness about violence against women as a violation of

women's enjoyment of their human rights and mobilize local communities to use appropriate gender-sensitive traditional and innovative methods of conflict resolution;

(f) Recognize, support and promote the fundamental role of intermediate institutions, such as primary health-care centers, family-planning centers, existing school health services, mother and baby protection services, centers for migrant families and so forth in the field of information and education related to abuse;

(g) Organize and fund information campaigns and educational and training programs in order to sensitize girls and boys and women and men to the personal and social detrimental effects of violence in the family, community and society; teach them how to communicate without violence and promote training for victims and potential victims so that they can protect themselves and others against such violence;

(h) Disseminate information on the assistance available to women and families who are victims of violence;

(i) Provide, fund and encourage counseling and rehabilitation programs for the perpetrators of violence and promote research to further efforts concerning such counseling and rehabilitation so as to prevent the recurrence of such violence;

(j) Raise awareness of the responsibility of the media in promoting non stereotyped images of women and men, as well as in eliminating patterns of media presentation that generate violence, and encourage those responsible for media content to establish professional guidelines and codes of conduct; also raise awareness of the important role of the media in informing and educating people about the causes and effects of violence against women and in stimulating public debate on the topic.

126. By Governments, employers, trade unions, community and youth organizations and non-governmental organizations, as appropriate:

(a) Develop programs and procedures to eliminate sexual harassment and other forms of violence against women in all educational institutions, workplaces and elsewhere;

(b) Develop programs and procedures to educate and raise awareness of acts of violence against women that constitute a crime and a violation of the human rights of women;

(c) Develop counseling, healing and support programs for girls, adolescents and young women who have been or are involved in abusive relationships, particularly those who live in homes or institutions where abuse occurs;

(d) Take special measures to eliminate violence against women, particularly those in vulnerable situations, such as young women, refugee, displaced and internally displaced women, women with disabilities and women migrant workers, including enforcing any existing legislation and developing,

as appropriate, new legislation for women migrant workers in both send-ing and receiving countries.

127. By the Secretary-General of the United Nations: Provide the Special Rapporteur of the Commission on Human Rights on vio-lence against women with all necessary assistance, in particular the staff and resources required to perform all mandated functions, es-pecially in carrying out and following up on missions undertaken either separately or jointly with other special rapporteurs and working groups, and adequate assistance for periodic consultations with the Committee on the Elimination of Discrimination against Women and all treaty bodies.

128. By Governments, international organizations and non-governmental organizations: Encourage the dissemination and im-plementation of the UNHCR Guidelines on the Protection of Refu-gee Women and the UNHCR Guidelines on the Prevention of and Response to Sexual Violence against Refugees.

STRATEGIC OBJECTIVE D.2.

> *Study the causes and consequences of violence against women and the effectiveness of preventive measures*

Actions to be taken

129. By Governments, regional organizations, the United Nations, other international organizations, research institutions, women's and youth organizations and non-governmental organizations, as ap-propriate:

(a) Promote research, collect data and compile statistics, especially concerning domestic violence relating to the prevalence of different forms of violence against women, and encourage research into the causes, nature, seriousness and consequences of violence against women and the effectiveness of measures implemented to prevent and redress violence against women;

(b) Disseminate findings of research and studies widely;

(c) Support and initiate research on the impact of violence, such as rape, on women and girl children, and make the resulting information and statistics available to the public;

(d) Encourage the media to examine the impact of gender role stereotypes, in-cluding those perpetuated by commercial advertisements which foster gen-der-based violence and inequalities, and how they are transmitted during the life cycle, and take measures to eliminate these negative images with a view to promoting a violence-free society.

> *Eliminate trafficking in women and assist victims of violence due to prostitution and trafficking*

Actions to be taken

130. By Governments of countries of origin, transit and destination, regional and international organizations, as appropriate:

(a) Consider the ratification and enforcement of international conventions on trafficking in persons and on slavery;

(b) Take appropriate measures to address the root factors, including external factors, that encourage trafficking in women and girls for prostitution and other forms of commercialized sex, forced marriages and forced labor in order to eliminate trafficking in women, including by strengthening existing legislation with a view to providing better protection of the rights of women and girls and to punishing the perpetrators, through both criminal and civil measures;

(c) Step up cooperation and concerted action by all relevant law enforcement authorities and institutions with a view to dismantling national, regional and international networks in trafficking;

(d) Allocate resources to provide comprehensive programs designed to heal and rehabilitate into society victims of trafficking, including through job training, legal assistance and confidential health care, and take measures to cooperate with non-governmental organizations to provide for the social, medical and psychological care of the victims of trafficking;

(e) Develop educational and training programs and policies and consider enacting legislation aimed at preventing sex tourism and trafficking, giving special emphasis to the protection of young women and children.

Chapter IV. E

WOMEN AND ARMED CONFLICT

131. An environment that maintains world peace and promotes and protects human rights, democracy and the peaceful settlement of disputes, in accordance with the principles of non-threat or use of force against territorial integrity or political independence and of respect for sovereignty as set forth in the Charter of the United Nations, is an important factor for the advancement of women. Peace is inextricably linked with equality between women and men and development. Armed and other types of conflicts and terrorism and hostage-taking still persist in many parts of the world. Aggression, foreign occupation, ethnic and other types of conflicts are an ongoing reality affecting women and men in nearly every region. Gross and systematic violations and situations that constitute serious obstacles to the full enjoyment of human rights continue to occur in different parts of the world. Such violations and obstacles include, as well as torture and cruel, inhuman and degrading treatment or punishment, summary and arbitrary executions, disappearances, arbitrary detentions, all forms of racism and racial discrimination, foreign occupation and alien domination, xenophobia, poverty, hunger and other denials of economic, social and cultural rights, religious intolerance, terrorism, discrimination against women and lack of the rule of law. International humanitarian law, prohibiting attacks on civilian populations, as such, is at times systematically ignored and human rights are often violated in connection with situations of armed conflict, affecting the civilian population, especially women, children, the elderly and the disabled. Violations of the human rights of women in situations of armed conflict are violations of the fundamental principles of international human rights and humanitarian law. Massive violations of human rights, especially in the form of genocide, ethnic cleansing as a strategy of war and its consequences, and rape, including systematic rape of women in war situations, creating a mass exodus of refugees and displaced persons, are abhorrent practices that are strongly condemned and must be stopped immediately, while perpetrators of such crimes must be punished. Some of these situations of armed conflict have their origin in the conquest or colonization of a country by another State and the perpetuation of that colonization through state and military repression.

132. The Geneva Convention relative to the Protection of Civilian Persons in Time of War, of 1949, and the Additional Protocols of 1977[24] provide that women shall especially be protected against any attack on their honor, in particular against humiliating and degrading treatment, rape, enforced prostitution or any form of indecent assault. The Vienna Declaration and Program of Action, adopted by the World Conference on Human Rights, states that "violations of the human rights of women in situations of armed conflict are violations of the fundamental principles of international human rights and humanitarian law".[25] All violations of this kind, including in particular murder, rape, including systematic rape, sexual slavery and forced pregnancy require a particularly effective response. Gross and systematic violations and situations that constitute serious obstacles to the full enjoyment of human rights continue to occur in different parts of the world. Such violations and obstacles include, as well as torture and cruel, inhuman and degrading treatment or summary and arbitrary detention, all forms of racism, racial discrimination, xenophobia, denial of economic, social and cultural rights and religious intolerance.

133. Violations of human rights in situations of armed conflict and military occupation are violations of the fundamental principles of international human rights and humanitarian law as embodied in international human rights instruments and in the Geneva Conventions of 1949 and the Additional Protocols thereto. Gross human rights violations and policies of ethnic cleansing in war-torn and occupied areas continue to be carried out. These practices have created, *inter alia*, a mass flow of refugees and other displaced persons in need of international protection and internally displaced persons, the majority of whom are women, adolescent girls and children. Civilian victims, mostly women and children, often outnumber casualties among combatants. In addition, women often become caregivers for injured combatants and find themselves, as a result of conflict, unexpectedly cast as sole manager of household, sole parent, and caretaker of elderly relatives.

134. In a world of continuing instability and violence, the implementation of cooperative approaches to peace and security is urgently needed. The equal access and full participation of women in power structures and their full involvement in all efforts for the prevention and resolution of conflicts are essential for the maintenance and promotion of peace and security. Although women have begun to play an important role in conflict resolution, peace-keeping and defense and foreign affairs mechanisms, they are still underrepresented in decision-making positions. If women are to play an equal part in securing and maintaining peace, they must be empowered

politically and economically and represented adequately at all levels of decision-making.

135. While entire communities suffer the consequences of armed conflict and terrorism, women and girls are particularly affected because of their status in society and their sex. Parties to conflict often rape women with impunity, sometimes using systematic rape as a tactic of war and terrorism. The impact of violence against women and violation of the human rights of women in such situations is experienced by women of all ages, who suffer displacement, loss of home and property, loss or involuntary disappearance of close relatives, poverty and family separation and disintegration, and who are victims of acts of murder, terrorism, torture, involuntary disappearance, sexual slavery, rape, sexual abuse and forced pregnancy in situations of armed conflict, especially as a result of policies of ethnic cleansing and other new and emerging forms of violence. This is compounded by the life-long social, economic and psychologically traumatic consequences of armed conflict and foreign occupation and alien domination.

136. Women and children constitute some 80 per cent of the world's millions of refugees and other displaced persons, including internally displaced persons. They are threatened by deprivation of property, goods and services and deprivation of their right to return to their homes of origin as well as by violence and insecurity. Particular attention should be paid to sexual violence against uprooted women and girls employed as a method of persecution in systematic campaigns of terror and intimidation and forcing members of a particular ethnic, cultural or religious group to flee their homes. Women may also be forced to flee as a result of a well founded fear of persecution for reasons enumerated in the 1951 Convention relating to the Status of Refugees and the 1967 Protocol, including persecution through sexual violence or other gender-related persecution, and they continue to be vulnerable to violence and exploitation while in flight, in countries of asylum and resettlement and during and after repatriation. Women often experience difficulty in some countries of asylum in being recognized as refugees when the claim is based on such persecution.

137. Refugee, displaced and migrant women in most cases display strength, endurance and resourcefulness and can contribute positively to countries of resettlement or to their country of origin on their return. They need to be appropriately involved in decisions that affect them.

138. Many women's non-governmental organizations have called for reductions in military expenditures world wide, as well as in international trade and trafficking in and the proliferation of weapons.

Those affected most negatively by conflict and excessive military spending are people living in poverty, who are deprived because of the lack of investment in basic services. Women living in poverty, particularly rural women, also suffer because of the use of arms that are particularly injurious or have indiscriminate effects. There are more than 100 million anti-personnel land-mines scattered in 64 countries globally. The negative impact on development of excessive military expenditures, the arms trade, and investment for arms production and acquisition must be addressed. At the same time, maintenance of national security and peace is an important factor for economic growth and development and the empowerment of women.

139. During times of armed conflict and the collapse of communities, the role of women is crucial. They often work to preserve social order in the midst of armed and other conflicts. Women make an important but often unrecognized contribution as peace educators both in their families and in their societies.

140. Education to foster a culture of peace that upholds justice and tolerance for all nations and peoples is essential to attaining lasting peace and should be begun at an early age. It should include elements of conflict resolution, mediation, reduction of prejudice and respect for diversity.

141. In addressing armed or other conflicts, an active and visible policy of mainstreaming a gender perspective into all policies and programs should be promoted so that before decisions are taken an analysis is made of the effects on women and men, respectively.

STRATEGIC OBJECTIVE E. 1.

> ✎ *Increase the participation of women in conflict resolution at decision-making levels and protect women living in situations of armed and other conflicts or under foreign occupation*

Actions to be taken

142. By Governments and international and regional intergovernmental institutions:

(*a*) Take action to promote equal participation of women and equal opportunities for women to participate in all forums and peace activities at all levels, particularly at the decision-making level, including in the United Nations Secretariat with due regard to equitable geographical distribution in accordance with Article 101 of the Charter of the United Nations;

(*b*) Integrate a gender perspective in the resolution of armed or other conflicts and foreign occupation and aim for gender balance when nominating or promoting candidates for judicial and other positions in all relevant international bodies, such as the United Nations International Tribunals for the former Yugoslavia and for Rwanda and the International Court of Justice, as well as in other bodies related to the peaceful settlement of disputes;

(c) Ensure that these bodies are able to address gender issues properly by providing appropriate training to prosecutors, judges and other officials in handling cases involving rape, forced pregnancy in situations of armed conflict, indecent assault and other forms of violence against women in armed conflicts, including terrorism, and integrate a gender perspective into their work.

STRATEGIC OBJECTIVE E. 2.

> ✎ *Reduce excessive military expenditures and control the availability of armaments*

Actions to be taken

143. By Governments:

(a) Increase and hasten, as appropriate, subject to national security considerations, the conversion of military resources and related industries to development and peaceful purposes;

(b) Undertake to explore new ways of generating new public and private financial resources, *inter alia*, through the appropriate reduction of excessive military expenditures, including global military expenditures, trade in arms and investment for arms production and acquisition, taking into consideration national security requirements, so as to permit the possible allocation of additional funds for social and economic development, in particular for the advancement of women;

(c) Take action to investigate and punish members of the police, security and armed forces and others who perpetrate acts of violence against women, violations of international humanitarian law and violations of the human rights of women in situations of armed conflict;

(d) While acknowledging legitimate national defense needs, recognize and address the dangers to society of armed conflict and the negative effect of excessive military expenditures, trade in arms, especially those arms that are particularly injurious or have indiscriminate effects, and excessive investment for arms production and acquisition; similarly, recognize the need to combat illicit arms trafficking, violence, crime, the production and use of and trafficking in illicit drugs, and trafficking in women and children;

(e) Recognizing that women and children are particularly affected by the indiscriminate use of anti-personnel land-mines:

(i) Undertake to work actively towards ratification, if they have not already done so, of the 1981 Convention on Prohibitions or Restrictions on the

Use of Certain Conventional Weapons Which May Be Deemed to Be Excessively Injurious or to Have Indiscriminate Effects, particularly the Protocol on Prohibitions or Restrictions on the Use of Mines, Booby Traps and Other Devices(Protocol II)[26] with a view to universal ratification by the year 2000;

(ii)Undertake to strongly consider strengthening the Convention to promote a reduction in the casualties and intense suffering caused to the civilian population by the indiscriminate use of land-mines;

(iii)Undertake to promote assistance in mine clearance, notably by facilitating, in respect of the means of mine-clearing, the exchange of information, the transfer of technology and the promotion of scientific research;

(iv)Within the United Nations context, undertake to support efforts to coordinate a common response program of assistance in de-mining without unnecessary discrimination;

(v) Adopt at the earliest possible date, if they have not already done so, a moratorium on the export of anti-personnel land-mines, including to non-governmental entities, noting with satisfaction that many States have already declared moratoriums on the export, transfer or sale of such mines;

(vi)Undertake to encourage further international efforts to seek solutions to the problems caused by antipersonnel land-mines, with a view to their eventual elimination, recognizing that States can move most effectively towards this goal as viable and humane alternatives are developed;

(f) Recognizing the leading role that women have played in the peace movement:

(i) Work actively towards general and complete disarmament under strict and effective international control;

(ii)Support negotiations on the conclusion, without delay, of a universal and multilaterally and effectively verifiable comprehensive nuclear-test-ban treaty that contributes to nuclear disarmament and the prevention of the proliferation of nuclear weapons in all its aspects;

(iii)Pending the entry into force of a comprehensive nuclear-test-ban treaty, exercise the utmost restraint in respect of nuclear testing.

STRATEGIC OBJECTIVE E.3.

> ∞ *Promote non-violent forms of conflict resolution and reduce the incidence of human rights abuse in conflict situations*

Actions to be taken

144. By Governments:

(a) Consider the ratification of or accession to international instruments containing provisions relative to the protection of women and children in armed conflicts, including the Geneva Convention relative to the Protection of Civilian Persons in Time of War, of 1949, the Protocols Additional to the Geneva Conventions of 1949 relating to the Protection of Victims of International Armed Conflicts(Protocol I) and to the Protection of Victims of Non-International Armed Conflicts(Protocol II);[24]

(b) Respect fully the norms of international humanitarian law in armed conflicts and take all measures required for the protection of women and children, in particular against rape, forced prostitution and any other form of indecent assault;

(c) Strengthen the role of women and ensure equal representation of women at all decision-making levels in national and international institutions which may make or influence policy with regard to matters related to peace keeping, preventive diplomacy and related activities and in all stages of peace mediation and negotiations, taking note of the specific recommendations of the Secretary-General in his strategic plan of action for the improvement of the status of women in the Secretariat(1995-2000)(A/49/587, sect. IV).

145. By Governments and international and regional organizations:

(a) Reaffirm the right of self-determination of all peoples, in particular of peoples under colonial or other forms of alien domination or foreign occupation, and the importance of the effective realization of this right, as enunciated, *inter alia*, in the Vienna Declaration and Program of Action,[2] adopted by the World Conference on Human Rights;

(b) Encourage diplomacy, negotiation and peaceful settlement of disputes in accordance with the Charter of the United Nations, in particular Article 2, paragraphs 3 and 4 thereof;

(c) Urge the identification and condemnation of the systematic practice of rape and other forms of inhuman and degrading treatment of women as a deliberate instrument of war and ethnic cleansing and take steps to ensure that full assistance is provided to the victims of such abuse for their physical and mental rehabilitation;

(d) Reaffirm that rape in the conduct of armed conflict constitutes a war crime and under certain circumstances it constitutes a crime against humanity and an act of genocide as defined in the Convention on the Prevention and Punishment of the Crime of Genocide;[27] take all measures required for the protection of women and children from such acts and strengthen mechanisms to investigate and punish all those responsible and bring the perpetrators to justice;

(e) Uphold and reinforce standards set out in international humanitarian law and international human rights instruments to prevent all acts of violence against women in situations of armed and other conflicts; undertake a full investigation of all acts of violence against women committed during war, including rape, in particular systematic rape, forced prostitution and other forms of indecent assault and sexual slavery; prosecute all criminals responsible for war crimes against women and provide full redress to women victims;

(f) Call upon the international community to condemn and act against all forms and manifestations of terrorism;

(g) Take into account gender-sensitive concerns in developing training programs for all relevant personnel on international humanitarian law and human rights awareness and recommend such training for those involved in United Nations peace-keeping and humanitarian aid, with a view to preventing violence against women, in particular;

(h) Discourage the adoption of and refrain from any unilateral measure not in accordance with international law and the Charter of the United Nations, that impedes the full achievement of economic and social development by the population of the affected countries, in particular women and children, that hinders their well-being and that creates obstacles to the full enjoyment of their human rights, including the right of everyone to a standard of living adequate for their health and well-being and their right to food, medical care and the necessary social services. This Conference reaffirms that food and medicine must not be used as a tool for political pressure;

(i) Take measures in accordance with international law with a view to alleviating the negative impact of economic sanctions on women and children.

STRATEGIC OBJECTIVE E.4.

> **Promote women's contribution to fostering a culture of peace**

Actions to be taken

146. By Governments, international and regional intergovernmental institutions and non-governmental organizations:

(a) Promote peaceful conflict resolution and peace, reconciliation and tolerance through education, training, community actions and youth exchange programs, in particular for young women;

(b) Encourage the further development of peace research, involving the participation of women, to examine the impact of armed conflict on women and children and the nature and contribution of women's participation in national, regional and international peace movements; engage in research and identify innovative mechanisms for containing violence and for conflict resolution for public dissemination and for use by women and men;

(c) Develop and disseminate research on the physical, psychological, economic and social effects of armed conflicts on women, particularly young women and girls, with a view to developing policies and programs to address the consequences of conflicts;

(*d*) Consider establishing educational programs for girls and boys to foster a culture of peace, focusing on conflict resolution by non-violent means and the promotion of tolerance.

STRATEGIC OBJECTIVE E. 5.

> ❧ *Provide protection, assistance and training to refugee women, other displaced women in need of international protection and internally displaced women*

Actions to be taken

147. By Governments, intergovernmental and non-governmental organizations and other institutions involved in providing protection, assistance and training to refugee women, other displaced women in need of international protection and internally displaced women, including the Office of the United Nations High Commissioner for Refugees and the World Food Program, as appropriate:

(*a*) Take steps to ensure that women are fully involved in the planning, design, implementation, monitoring and evaluation of all short-term and long-term projects and programs providing assistance to refugee women, other displaced women in need of international protection and internally displaced women, including the management of refugee camps and resources; ensure that refugee and displaced women and girls have direct access to the services provided;

(*b*) Offer adequate protection and assistance to women and children displaced within their country and find solutions to the root causes of their displacement with a view to preventing it and, when appropriate, facilitate their return or resettlement;

(*c*) Take steps to protect the safety and physical integrity of refugee women, other displaced women in need of international protection and internally displaced women during their displacement and upon their return to their communities of origin, including programs of rehabilitation; take effective measures to protect from violence women who are refugees or displaced; hold an impartial and thorough investigation of any such violations and bring those responsible to justice;

(*d*) While fully respecting and strictly observing the principle of non refoulement of refugees, take all the necessary steps to ensure the right of refugee and displaced women to return voluntarily to their place of origin in safety and with dignity, and their right to protection after their return;

(*e*) Take measures, at the national level with international cooperation, as appropriate, in accordance with the Charter of the United Nations, to find lasting solutions to questions related to internally displaced women, including their right to voluntary and safe return to their home of origin;

(f) Ensure that the international community and its international organizations provide financial and other resources for emergency relief and other longer-term assistance that takes into account the specific needs, resources and potentials of refugee women, other displaced women in need of international protection and internally displaced women; in the provision of protection and assistance, take all appropriate measures to eliminate discrimination against women and girls in order to ensure equal access to appropriate and adequate food, water and shelter, education, and social and health services, including reproductive health care and maternity care and services to combat tropical diseases;

(g) Facilitate the availability of educational materials in the appropriate language - in emergency situations also - in order to minimize disruption of schooling among refugee and displaced children;

(h) Apply international norms to ensure equal access and equal treatment of women and men in refugee determination procedures and the granting of asylum, including full respect and strict observation of the principle of non-refoulement through, *inter alia*, bringing national immigration regulations into conformity with relevant international instruments, and consider recognizing as refugees those women whose claim to refugee status is based upon the well-founded fear of persecution for reasons enumerated in the 1951 Convention[28] and the 1967 Protocol[29] relating to the Status of Refugees, including persecution through sexual violence or other gender related persecution, and provide access to specially trained officers, including female officers, to interview women regarding sensitive or painful experiences, such as sexual assault;

(i) Support and promote efforts by States towards the development of criteria and guidelines on responses to persecution specifically aimed at women, by sharing information on States' initiatives to develop such criteria and guidelines and by monitoring to ensure their fair and consistent application;

(j) Promote the self-reliant capacities of refugee women, other displaced women in need of international protection and internally displaced women and provide programs for women, particularly young women, in leadership and decision-making within refugee and returnee communities;

(k) Ensure that the human rights of refugee and displaced women are protected and that refugee and displaced women are made aware of these rights; ensure that the vital importance of family reunification is recognized;

(l) Provide, as appropriate, women who have been determined refugees with access to vocational/professional training programs, including language training, small-scale enterprise development training and planning and counseling on all forms of violence against women, which should include rehabilitation programs for victims of torture and trauma; Governments and other donors should contribute adequately to assistance programs for

refugee women, other displaced women in need of international protection and internally displaced women, taking into account in particular the effects on the host countries of the increasing requirements of large refugee populations and the need to widen the donor base and to achieve greater burden-sharing;

(m) Raise public awareness of the contribution made by refugee women to their countries of resettlement, promote understanding of their human rights and of their needs and abilities and encourage mutual understanding and acceptance through educational programs promoting cross-cultural and interracial harmony;

(n) Provide basic and support services to women who are displaced from their place of origin as a result of terrorism, violence, drug trafficking or other reasons linked to violence situations;

(o) Develop awareness of the human rights of women and provide, as appropriate, human rights education and training to military and police personnel operating in areas of armed conflict and areas where there are refugees.

148. By Governments:

(a) Disseminate and implement the UNHCR Guidelines on the Protection of Refugee Women and the UNHCR Guidelines on Evaluation and Care of Victims of Trauma and Violence, or provide similar guidance, in close cooperation with refugee women and in all sectors of refugee programs;

(b) Protect women and children who migrate as family members from abuse or denial of their human rights by sponsors and consider extending their stay, should the family relationship dissolve, within the limits of national legislation.

STRATEGIC OBJECTIVE E. 6.

> ❧ *Provide assistance to the women of the colonies and non-self-governing territories*

Actions to be taken

149. By Governments and intergovernmental and non-governmental organizations:

(a) Support and promote the implementation of the right of self-determination of all peoples as enunciated, *inter alia*, in the Vienna Declaration and PROGRAM OF ACTION by providing special programs in leadership and in training for decision-making;

(b) Raise public awareness, as appropriate, through the mass media, education at all levels and special programs to create a better understanding of the situation of women of the colonies and non self-governing territories.

Chapter IV. F

WOMEN AND THE ECONOMY

150. There are considerable differences in women's and men's access to and opportunities to exert power over economic structures in their societies. In most parts of the world, women are virtually absent from or are poorly represented in economic decision-making, including the formulation of financial, monetary, commercial and other economic policies, as well as tax systems and rules governing pay. Since it is often within the framework of such policies that individual men and women make their decisions, *inter alia*, on how to divide their time between remunerated and unremunerated work, the actual development of these economic structures and policies has a direct impact on women's and men's access to economic resources, their economic power and consequently the extent of equality between them at the individual and family levels as well as in society as a whole.

151. In many regions, women's participation in remunerated work in the formal and non-formal labor market has increased significantly and has changed during the past decade. While women continue to work in agriculture and fisheries, they have also become increasingly involved in micro, small and medium-sized enterprises and, in some cases, have become more dominant in the expanding informal sector. Due to, *inter alia*, difficult economic situations and a lack of bargaining power resulting from gender inequality, many women have been forced to accept low pay and poor working conditions and thus have often become preferred workers. On the other hand, women have entered the work-force increasingly by choice when they have become aware of and demanded their rights. Some have succeeded in entering and advancing in the workplace and improving their pay and working conditions. However, women have been particularly affected by the economic situation and restructuring processes, which have changed the nature of employment and, in some cases, have led to a loss of jobs, even for professional and skilled women. In addition, many women have entered the informal sector owing to the lack of other opportunities. Women's participation and gender concerns are still largely absent from and should be integrated in the policy formulation process of the multilateral institutions that define the terms and, in cooperation with

Governments, set the goals of structural adjustment programs, loans and grants.

152. Discrimination in education and training, hiring and remuneration, promotion and horizontal mobility practices, as well as inflexible working conditions, lack of access to productive resources and inadequate sharing of family responsibilities, combined with a lack of or insufficient services such as child care, continue to restrict employment, economic, professional and other opportunities and mobility for women and make their involvement stressful. Moreover, attitudinal obstacles inhibit women's participation in developing economic policy and in some regions restrict the access of women and girls to education and training for economic management.

153. Women's share in the labor force continues to rise and almost everywhere women are working more outside the household, although there has not been a parallel lightening of responsibility for unremunerated work in the household and community. Women's income is becoming increasingly necessary to households of all types. In some regions, there has been a growth in women's entrepreneurship and other self-reliant activities, particularly in the informal sector. In many countries, women are the majority of workers in non-standard work, such as temporary, casual, multiple part-time, contract and home-based employment.

154. Women migrant workers, including domestic workers, contribute to the economy of the sending country through their remittances and also to the economy of the receiving country through their participation in the labor force. However, in many receiving countries, migrant women experience higher levels of unemployment compared with both non-migrant workers and male migrant workers.

155. Insufficient attention to gender analysis has meant that women's contributions and concerns remain too often ignored in economic structures, such as financial markets and institutions, labor markets, economics as an academic discipline, economic and social infrastructure, taxation and social security systems, as well as in families and households. As a result, many policies and programs may continue to contribute to inequalities between women and men. Where progress has been made in integrating gender perspectives, program and policy effectiveness has also been enhanced.

156. Although many women have advanced in economic structures, for the majority of women, particularly those who face additional barriers, continuing obstacles have hindered their ability to achieve economic autonomy and to ensure sustainable livelihoods for themselves and their dependents. Women are active in a variety of

economic areas, which they often combine, ranging from wage labor and subsistence farming and fishing to the informal sector. However, legal and customary barriers to ownership of or access to land, natural resources, capital, credit, technology and other means of production, as well as wage differentials, contribute to impeding the economic progress of women. Women contribute to development not only through remunerated work but also through a great deal of unremunerated work. On the one hand, women participate in the production of goods and services for the market and household consumption, in agriculture, food production or family enterprises. Though included in the United Nations System of National Accounts and therefore in international standards for labor statistics, this unremunerated work particularly that related to agriculture is often undervalued and unrecorded. On the other hand, women still also perform the great majority of unremunerated domestic work and community work, such as caring for children and older persons, preparing food for the family, protecting the environment and providing voluntary assistance to vulnerable and disadvantaged individuals and groups. This work is often not measured in quantitative terms and is not valued in national accounts. Women's contribution to development is seriously underestimated, and thus its social recognition is limited. The full visibility of the type, extent and distribution of this unremunerated work will also contribute to a better sharing of responsibilities.

157. Although some new employment opportunities have been created for women as a result of the globalization of the economy, there are also trends that have exacerbated inequalities between women and men. At the same time, globalization, including economic integration, can create pressures on the employment situation of women to adjust to new circumstances and to find new sources of employment as patterns of trade change. More analysis needs to be done of the impact of globalization on women's economic status.

158. These trends have been characterized by low wages, little or no labor standards protection, poor working conditions, particularly with regard to women's occupational health and safety, low skill levels, and a lack of job security and social security, in both the formal and informal sectors. Women's unemployment is a serious and increasing problem in many countries and sectors. Young workers in the informal and rural sectors and migrant female workers remain the least protected by labor and immigration laws. Women, particularly those who are heads of households with young children, are limited in their employment opportunities for reasons

that include inflexible working conditions and inadequate sharing, by men and by society, of family responsibilities.

159. In countries that are undergoing fundamental political, economic and social transformation, the skills of women, if better utilized, could constitute a major contribution to the economic life of their respective countries. Their input should continue to be developed and supported and their potential further realized.

160. Lack of employment in the private sector and reductions in public services and public service jobs have affected women disproportionately. In some countries, women take on more unpaid work, such as the care of children and those who are ill or elderly, compensating for lost household income, particularly when public services are not available. In many cases, employment creation strategies have not paid sufficient attention to occupations and sectors where women predominate; nor have they adequately promoted the access of women to those occupations and sectors that are traditionally male.

161. For those women in paid work, many experience obstacles that prevent them from achieving their potential. While some are increasingly found in lower levels of management, attitudinal discrimination often prevents them from being promoted further. The experience of sexual harassment is an affront to a worker's dignity and prevents women from making a contribution commensurate with their abilities. The lack of a family-friendly work environment, including a lack of appropriate and affordable child care, and inflexible working hours further prevent women from achieving their full potential.

162. In the private sector, including transnational and national enterprises, women are largely absent from management and policy levels, denoting discriminatory hiring and promotion policies and practices. The unfavorable work environment as well as the limited number of employment opportunities available have led many women to seek alternatives. Women have increasingly become self-employed and owners and managers of micro, small and medium-scale enterprises. The expansion of the informal sector, in many countries, and of self-organized and independent enterprises is in large part due to women, whose collaborative, self-help and traditional practices and initiatives in production and trade represent a vital economic resource. When they gain access to and control over capital, credit and other resources, technology and training, women can increase production, marketing and income for sustainable development.

163. Taking into account the fact that continuing inequalities and noticeable progress coexist, rethinking employment policies is nec-

essary in order to integrate the gender perspective and to draw attention to a wider range of opportunities as well as to address any negative gender implications of current patterns of work and employment. To realize fully equality between women and men in their contribution to the economy, active efforts are required for equal recognition and appreciation of the influence that the work, experience, knowledge and values of both women and men have in society.

164. In addressing the economic potential and independence of women, Governments and other actors should promote an active and visible policy of mainstreaming a gender perspective in all policies and programs so that before decisions are taken, an analysis is made of the effects on women and men, respectively.

STRATEGIC OBJECTIVE F. 1.

> ✎ *Promote women's economic rights and independence, including access to employment, appropriate working conditions and control over economic resources*

Actions to be taken

165. By Governments:

(a) Enact and enforce legislation to guarantee the rights of women and men to equal pay for equal work or work of equal value;

(b) Adopt and implement laws against discrimination based on sex in the labor market, especially considering older women workers, hiring and promotion, the extension of employment benefits and social security, and working conditions;

(c) Eliminate discriminatory practices by employers and take appropriate measures in consideration of women's reproductive role and functions, such as the denial of employment and dismissal due to pregnancy or breast feeding, or requiring proof of contraceptive use, and take effective measures to ensure that pregnant women, women on maternity leave or women re-entering the labor market after childbearing are not discriminated against;

(d) Devise mechanisms and take positive action to enable women to gain access to full and equal participation in the formulation of policies and definition of structures through such bodies as ministries of finance and trade, national economic commissions, economic research institutes and other key agencies, as well as through their participation in appropriate international bodies;

(e) Undertake legislation and administrative reforms to give women equal rights with men to economic resources, including access to ownership and control over land and other forms of property, credit, inheritance, natural resources and appropriate new technology;

(f) Conduct reviews of national income and inheritance tax and social security systems to eliminate any existing bias against women;

(g) Seek to develop a more comprehensive knowledge of work and employment through, *inter alia*, efforts to measure and better understand the type, extent and distribution of unremunerated work, particularly work in caring for dependents and unremunerated work done for family farms or businesses, and encourage the sharing and dissemination of information on studies and experience in this field, including the development of methods for assessing its value in quantitative terms, for possible reflection in accounts that may be produced separately from, but consistent with, core national accounts;

(h) Review and amend laws governing the operation of financial institutions to ensure that they provide services to women and men on an equal basis;

(i) Facilitate, at appropriate levels, more open and transparent budget processes;

(j) Revise and implement national policies that support the traditional savings, credit and lending mechanisms for women;

(k) Seek to ensure that national policies related to international and regional trade agreements do not have an adverse impact on women's new and traditional economic activities;

(l) Ensure that all corporations, including transnational corporations, comply with national laws and codes, social security regulations, applicable international agreements, instruments and conventions, including those related to the environment, and other relevant laws;

(m) Adjust employment policies to facilitate the restructuring of work patterns in order to promote the sharing of family responsibilities;

(n) Establish mechanisms and other forums to enable women entrepreneurs and women workers to contribute to the formulation of policies and programs being developed by economic ministries and financial institutions;

(o) Enact and enforce equal opportunity laws, take positive action and ensure compliance by the public and private sectors through various means;

(p) Use gender-impact analyses in the development of macro and microeconomic and social policies in order to monitor such impact and restructure policies in cases where harmful impact occurs;

(q) Promote gender-sensitive policies and measures to empower women as equal partners with men in technical, managerial and entrepreneurial fields;

(r) Reform laws or enact national policies that support the establishment of labor laws to ensure the protection of all women workers, including safe work practices, the right to organize and access to justice.

STRATEGIC OBJECTIVE F. 2.

❧ *Facilitate women's equal access to resources, employment, markets and trade*

Actions to be taken

166. By Governments:

(a) Promote and support women's self-employment and the development of small enterprises, and strengthen women's access to credit and capital on appropriate terms equal to those of men through the scaling-up of institutions dedicated to promoting women's entrepreneurship, including, as appropriate, non-traditional and mutual credit schemes, as well as innovative linkages with financial institutions;

(b) Strengthen the incentive role of the State as employer to develop a policy of equal opportunities for women and men;

(c) Enhance, at the national and local levels, rural women's income generating potential by facilitating their equal access to and control over productive resources, land, credit, capital, property rights, development programs and cooperative structures;

(d) Promote and strengthen micro-enterprises, new small businesses, cooperative enterprises, expanded markets and other employment opportunities and, where appropriate, facilitate the transition from the informal to the formal sector, especially in rural areas;

(e) Create and modify programs and policies that recognize and strengthen women's vital role in food security and provide paid and unpaid women producers, especially those involved in food production, such as farming, fishing and aquaculture, as well as urban enterprises, with equal access to appropriate technologies, transportation, extension services, marketing and credit facilities at the local and community levels;

(f) Establish appropriate mechanisms and encourage intersectoral institutions that enable women's cooperatives to optimize access to necessary services;

(g) Increase the proportion of women extension workers and other government personnel who provide technical assistance or administer economic programs;

(h) Review, reformulate, if necessary, and implement policies, including business, commercial and contract law and government regulations, to ensure that they do not discriminate against micro, small and medium scale enterprises owned by women in rural and urban areas;

(i) Analyze, advise on, coordinate and implement policies that integrate the needs and interests of employed, self-employed and entrepreneurial women into sectoral and inter-ministerial policies, programs and budgets;

(j) Ensure equal access for women to effective job training, retraining, counseling and placement services that are not limited to traditional employment areas;

(k) Remove policy and regulatory obstacles faced by women in social and development programs that discourage private and individual initiative;

(l) Safeguard and promote respect for basic workers' rights, including the prohibition of forced labor and child labor, freedom of association and the right to organize and bargain collectively, equal remuneration for men and women for work of equal value and non-discrimination in employment, fully implementing the conventions of the International Labour Organization in the case of States Parties to those conventions and, taking into account the principles embodied in the case of those countries that are not parties to those conventions in order to achieve truly sustained economic growth and sustainable development.

167. By Governments, central banks and national development banks, and private banking institutions, as appropriate:

(a) Increase the participation of women, including women entrepreneurs, in advisory boards and other forums to enable women entrepreneurs from all sectors and their organizations to contribute to the formulation and review of policies and programs being developed by economic ministries and banking institutions;

(b) Mobilize the banking sector to increase lending and refinancing through incentives and the development of intermediaries that serve the needs of women entrepreneurs and producers in both rural and urban areas, and include women in their leadership, planning and decision-making;

(c) Structure services to reach rural and urban women involved in micro, small and medium-scale enterprises, with special attention to young women, low-income women, those belonging to ethnic and racial minorities, and indigenous women who lack access to capital and assets; and expand women's access to financial markets by identifying and encouraging financial supervisory and regulatory reforms that support financial institutions' direct and indirect efforts to better meet the credit and other financial needs of the micro, small and medium-scale enterprises of women;

(d) Ensure that women's priorities are included in public investment programs for economic infrastructure, such as water and sanitation, electrification and energy conservation, transport and road construction; promote greater involvement of women beneficiaries at the project planning and implementation stages to ensure access to jobs and contracts.

168. By Governments and non-governmental organizations:

(a) Pay special attention to women's needs when disseminating market, trade and resource information and provide appropriate training in these fields;

(b) Encourage community economic development strategies that build on partnerships among Governments, and encourage members of civil society to create jobs and address the social circumstances of individuals, families and communities.

169. By multilateral funders and regional development banks, as well as bilateral and private funding agencies, at the international, regional and subregional levels:

(a) Review, where necessary reformulate, and implement policies, programs and projects, to ensure that a higher proportion of resources reach women in rural and remote areas;

(b) Develop flexible funding arrangements to finance intermediary institutions that target women's economic activities, and promote self sufficiency and increased capacity in and profitability of women's economic enterprises;

(c) Develop strategies to consolidate and strengthen their assistance to the micro, small and medium-scale enterprise sector, in order to enhance the opportunities for women to participate fully and equally and work together to coordinate and enhance the effectiveness of this sector, drawing upon expertise and financial resources from within their own organizations as well as from bilateral agencies, Governments and non governmental organizations.

170. By international, multilateral and bilateral development cooperation organizations:

Support, through the provision of capital and/or resources, financial institutions that serve low-income, small and micro-scale women entrepreneurs and producers in both the formal and informal sectors.

171. By Governments and/or multilateral financial institutions:

Review rules and procedures of formal national and international financial institutions that obstruct replication of the Grameen Bank prototype, which provides credit facilities to rural women.

172. By international organizations:

Provide adequate support for programs and projects designed to promote sustainable and productive entrepreneurial activities among women, in particular the disadvantaged.

STRATEGIC OBJECTIVE F.3.

> ✎ *Provide business services, training and access to markets, information and technology, particularly to low-income women*

Actions to be taken

173. By Governments in cooperation with non-governmental organizations and the private sector:

(*a*) Provide public infrastructure to ensure equal market access for women and men entrepreneurs;

(*b*) Develop programs that provide training and retraining, particularly in new technologies, and affordable services to women in business management, product development, financing, production and quality control, marketing and the legal aspects of business;

(*c*) Provide outreach programs to inform low-income and poor women, particularly in rural and remote areas, of opportunities for market and technology access, and provide assistance in taking advantage of such opportunities;

(*d*) Create non-discriminatory support services, including investment funds for women's businesses, and target women, particularly low-income women, in trade promotion programs;

(*e*) Disseminate information about successful women entrepreneurs in both traditional and non-traditional economic activities and the skills necessary to achieve success, and facilitate networking and the exchange of information;

(*f*) Take measures to ensure equal access of women to ongoing training in the workplace, including unemployed women, single parents, women reentering the labor market after an extended temporary exit from employment owing to family responsibilities and other causes, and women displaced by new forms of production or by retrenchment, and increase incentives to enterprises to expand the number of vocational and training centers that provide training for women in non-traditional areas;

(*g*) Provide affordable support services, such as high-quality, flexible and affordable child-care services, that take into account the needs of working men and women.

174. By local, national, regional and international business organizations and non-governmental organizations concerned with women's issues: Advocate, at all levels, for the promotion and support of women's businesses and enterprises, including those in the informal sector, and the equal access of women to productive resources.

STRATEGIC OBJECTIVE F.4.

> ❧ *Strengthen women's economic capacity and commercial networks*

Actions to be taken

175. By Governments:

(*a*) Adopt policies that support business organizations, non-governmental organizations, cooperatives, revolving loan funds, credit unions, grass roots organizations, women's self-help groups and other groups in order to provide services to women entrepreneurs in rural and urban areas;

(*b*) Integrate a gender perspective into all economic restructuring and structural adjustment policies and design programs for women who are affected by economic restructuring, including structural adjustment programs, and for women who work in the informal sector;

(*c*) Adopt policies that create an enabling environment for women's self-help groups, workers' organizations and cooperatives through non conventional forms of support and by recognizing the right to freedom of association and the right to organize;

(*d*) Support programs that enhance the self-reliance of special groups of women, such as young women, women with disabilities, elderly women and women belonging to racial and ethnic minorities;

(*e*) Promote gender equality through the promotion of women's studies and through the use of the results of studies and gender research in all fields, including the economic, scientific and technological fields;

(*f*) Support the economic activities of indigenous women, taking into account their traditional knowledge, so as to improve their situation and development;

(*g*) Adopt policies to extend or maintain the protection of labor laws and social security provisions for those who do paid work in the home;(*h*) Recognize and encourage the contribution of research by women scientists and technologists;

(*i*) Ensure that policies and regulations do not discriminate against micro, small and medium-scale enterprises run by women.

176. By financial intermediaries, national training institutes, credit unions, non-governmental organizations, women's associations, professional organizations and the private sector, as appropriate:

(*a*) Provide, at the national, regional and international levels, training in a variety of business-related and financial management and technical skills to enable women, especially young women, to participate in economic policy-making at those levels;

(*b*) Provide business services, including marketing and trade information, product design and innovation, technology transfer and quality, to women's business enterprises, including those in export sectors of the economy;

(*c*) Promote technical and commercial links and establish joint ventures among women entrepreneurs at the national, regional and international levels to support community-based initiatives;

(*d*) Strengthen the participation of women, including marginalized women, in production and marketing cooperatives by providing marketing and financial support, especially in rural and remote areas;

(e) Promote and strengthen women's micro-enterprises, new small businesses, cooperative enterprises, expanded markets and other employment opportunities and, where appropriate, facilitate the transition from the informal to the formal sector, in rural and urban areas;

(f) Invest capital and develop investment portfolios to finance women's business enterprises;

(g) Give adequate attention to providing technical assistance, advisory services, training and retraining for women connected with the entry to the market economy;

(h) Support credit networks and innovative ventures, including traditional savings schemes;

(i) Provide networking arrangements for entrepreneurial women, including opportunities for the mentoring of inexperienced women by the more experienced;

(j) Encourage community organizations and public authorities to establish loan pools for women entrepreneurs, drawing on successful small-scale co-operative models.

177. By the private sector, including transnational and national corporations:

(a) Adopt policies and establish mechanisms to grant contracts on a non- discriminatory basis;

(b) Recruit women for leadership, decision-making and management and provide training programs, all on an equal basis with men;

(c) Observe national labor, environment, consumer, health and safety laws, particularly those that affect women.

STRATEGIC OBJECTIVE F.5.

> 🦐 *Eliminate occupational segregation and all forms of employment discrimination*

Actions to be taken

178. By Governments, employers, employees, trade unions and women's organizations:

(a) Implement and enforce laws and regulations and encourage voluntary codes of conduct that ensure that international labor standards, such as International Labour Organization Convention No. 100 on equal pay and workers' rights, apply equally to female and male workers;

(b) Enact and enforce laws and introduce implementing measures, including means of redress and access to justice in cases of non-compliance, to prohibit direct and indirect discrimination on grounds of sex, including by reference to marital or family status, in relation to access to employment,

conditions of employment, including training, promotion, health and safety, as well as termination of employment and social security of workers, including legal protection against sexual and racial harassment;

(c) Enact and enforce laws and develop workplace policies against gender discrimination in the labor market, especially considering older women workers, in hiring and promotion, and in the extension of employment benefits and social security, as well as regarding discriminatory working conditions and sexual harassment; mechanisms should be developed for the regular review and monitoring of such laws;

(d) Eliminate discriminatory practices by employers on the basis of women's reproductive roles and functions, including refusal of employment and dismissal of women due to pregnancy and breast-feeding responsibilities;

(e) Develop and promote employment programs and services for women entering and/or re-entering the labor market, especially poor urban, rural and young women, the self-employed and those negatively affected by structural adjustment;

(f) Implement and monitor positive public- and private-sector employment, equity and positive action programs to address systemic discrimination against women in the labor force, in particular women with disabilities and women belonging to other disadvantaged groups, with respect to hiring, retention and promotion, and vocational training of women in all sectors;

(g) Eliminate occupational segregation, especially by promoting the equal participation of women in highly skilled jobs and senior management positions, and through other measures, such as counseling and placement, that stimulate their on-the-job career development and upward mobility in the labor market, and by stimulating the diversification of occupational choices by both women and men; encourage women to take up non-traditional jobs, especially in science and technology, and encourage men to seek employment in the social sector;

(h) Recognize collective bargaining as a right and as an important mechanism for eliminating wage inequality for women and to improve working conditions;

(i) Promote the election of women trade union officials and ensure that trade union officials elected to represent women are given job protection and physical security in connection with the discharge of their functions;

(j) Ensure access to and develop special programs to enable women with disabilities to obtain and retain employment, and ensure access to education and training at all proper levels, in accordance with the Standard Rules on the Equalization of Opportunities for Persons with Disabilities; [30] adjust working conditions, to the extent possible, in order to suit the needs of women with disabilities, who should be assured legal protection against unfounded job loss on account of their disabilities;

(k) Increase efforts to close the gap between women's and men's pay, take steps to implement the principle of equal remuneration for equal work of equal value by strengthening legislation, including compliance with international labor laws and standards, and encourage job evaluation schemes with gender-neutral criteria;

(l) Establish and/or strengthen mechanisms to adjudicate matters relating to wage discrimination;

(m) Set specific target dates for eliminating all forms of child labor that are contrary to accepted international standards and ensure the full enforcement of relevant existing laws and, where appropriate, enact the legislation necessary to implement the Convention on the Rights of the Child and International Labour Organization standards, ensuring the protection of working children, in particular, street children, through the provision of appropriate health, education and other social services;

(n) Ensure that strategies to eliminate child labor also address the excessive demands made on some girls for unpaid work in their household and other households, where applicable;

(o) Review, analyze and, where appropriate, reformulate the wage structures in female-dominated professions, such as teaching, nursing and child care, with a view to raising their low status and earnings;

(p) Facilitate the productive employment of documented migrant women (including women who have been determined refugees according to the 1951 Convention relating to the Status of Refugees) through greater recognition of foreign education and credentials and by adopting an integrated approach to labor market training that incorporates language training.

STRATEGIC OBJECTIVE F.6.

✎ Promote harmonization of work and family responsibilities for women and men

Actions to be taken

179. By Governments:

(a) Adopt policies to ensure the appropriate protection of labor laws and social security benefits for part-time, temporary, seasonal and home-based workers; promote career development based on work conditions that harmonize work and family responsibilities;

(b) Ensure that full and part-time work can be freely chosen by women and men on an equal basis, and consider appropriate protection for atypical workers in terms of access to employment, working conditions and social security;

(c) Ensure, through legislation, incentives and/or encouragement, opportunities for women and men to take job-protected parental leave and to have pa-

rental benefits; promote the equal sharing of responsibilities for the family by men and women, including through appropriate legislation, incentives and/or encouragement, and also promote the facilitation of breast-feeding for working mothers;

(d) Develop policies, *inter alia*, in education to change attitudes that reinforce the division of labor based on gender in order to promote the concept of shared family responsibility for work in the home, particularly in relation to children and elder care;

(e) Improve the development of, and access to, technologies that facilitate occupational as well as domestic work, encourage self-support, generate income, transform gender-prescribed roles within the productive process and enable women to move out of low-paying jobs;

(f) Examine a range of policies and programs, including social security legislation and taxation systems, in accordance with national priorities and policies, to determine how to promote gender equality and flexibility in the way people divide their time between and derive benefits from education and training, paid employment, family responsibilities, volunteer activity and other socially useful forms of work, rest and leisure.

180. By Governments, the private sector and non-governmental organizations, trade unions and the United Nations, as appropriate:

(a) Adopt appropriate measures involving relevant governmental bodies and employers' and employees' associations so that women and men are able to take temporary leave from employment, have transferable employment and retirement benefits and make arrangements to modify work hours without sacrificing their prospects for development and advancement at work and in their careers;

(b) Design and provide educational programs through innovative media campaigns and school and community education programs to raise awareness on gender equality and non-stereotyped gender roles of women and men within the family; provide support services and facilities, such as on-site child care at workplaces and flexible working arrangements;

(c) Enact and enforce laws against sexual and other forms of harassment in all workplaces.

Chapter IV. G

WOMEN IN POWER AND DECISION-MAKING

181. *The Universal Declaration of Human Rights* states that everyone has the right to take part in the Government of his/her country. The empowerment and autonomy of women and the improvement of women's social, economic and political status is essential for the achievement of both transparent and accountable government and administration and sustainable development in all areas of life. The power relations that prevent women from leading fulfilling lives operate at many levels of society, from the most personal to the highly public. Achieving the goal of equal participation of women and men in decision-making will provide a balance that more accurately reflects the composition of society and is needed in order to strengthen democracy and promote its proper functioning. Equality in political decision-making performs a leverage function without which it is highly unlikely that a real integration of the equality dimension in government policy-making is feasible. In this respect, women's equal participation in political life plays a pivotal role in the general process of the advancement of women. Women's equal participation in decision-making is not only a demand for simple justice or democracy but can also be seen as a necessary condition for women's interests to be taken into account. Without the active participation of women and the incorporation of women's perspective at all levels of decision-making, the goals of equality, development and peace cannot be achieved.

182. Despite the widespread movement towards democratization in most countries, women are largely underrepresented at most levels of government, especially in ministerial and other executive bodies, and have made little progress in attaining political power in legislative bodies or in achieving the target endorsed by the Economic and Social Council of having 30 per cent women in positions at decision-making levels by 1995. Globally, only 10 per cent of the members of legislative bodies and a lower percentage of ministerial positions are now held by women. Indeed, some countries, including those that are undergoing fundamental political, economic and social changes, have seen a significant decrease in the number of women represented in legislative bodies. Although women make up

at least half of the electorate in almost all countries and have attained the right to vote and hold office in almost all States Members of the United Nations, women continue to be seriously underrepresented as candidates for public office. The traditional working patterns of many political parties and government structures continue to be barriers to women's participation in public life. Women may be discouraged from seeking political office by discriminatory attitudes and practices, family and child-care responsibilities, and the high cost of seeking and holding public office. Women in politics and decision-making positions in Governments and legislative bodies contribute to redefining political priorities, placing new items on the political agenda that reflect and address women's gender-specific concerns, values and experiences, and providing new perspectives on mainstream political issues.

183. Women have demonstrated considerable leadership in community and informal organizations, as well as in public office. However, socialization and negative stereotyping of women and men, including stereotyping through the media, reinforces the tendency for political decision-making to remain the domain of men. Likewise, the underrepresentation of women in decision-making positions in the areas of art, culture, sports, the media, education, religion and the law have prevented women from having a significant impact on many key institutions.

184. Owing to their limited access to the traditional avenues to power, such as the decision-making bodies of political parties, employer organizations and trade unions, women have gained access to power through alternative structures, particularly in the non-governmental organization sector. Through non-governmental organizations and grass-roots organizations, women have been able to articulate their interests and concerns and have placed women's issues on the national, regional and international agendas.

185. Inequality in the public arena can often start with discriminatory attitudes and practices and unequal power relations between women and men within the family, as defined in paragraph 29 above. The unequal division of labor and responsibilities within households based on unequal power relations also limits women's potential to find the time and develop the skills required for participation in decision-making in wider public forums. A more equal sharing of those responsibilities between women and men not only provides a better quality of life for women and their daughters but also enhances their opportunities to shape and design public policy, practice and expenditure so that their interests may be recognized and addressed. Non-formal networks and patterns of decision-making at the local community level that reflect a dominant male ethos re-

strict women's ability to participate equally in political, economic and social life.

186. The low proportion of women among economic and political decision makers at the local, national, regional and international levels reflects structural and attitudinal barriers that need to be addressed through positive measures. Governments, transnational and national corporations, the mass media, banks, academic and scientific institutions, and regional and international organizations, including those in the United Nations system, do not make full use of women's talents as top-level managers, policy makers, diplomats and negotiators.

187. The equitable distribution of power and decision-making at all levels is dependent on Governments and other actors undertaking statistical gender analysis and mainstreaming a gender perspective in policy development and the implementation of programs. Equality in decision-making is essential to the empowerment of women. In some countries, affirmative action has led to 33.3 per cent or larger representation in local and national Governments.

188. National, regional and international statistical institutions still have insufficient knowledge of how to present the issues related to the equal treatment of women and men in the economic and social spheres. In particular, there is insufficient use of existing databases and methodologies in the important sphere of decision-making.

189. In addressing the inequality between men and women in the sharing of power and decision-making at all levels, Governments and other actors should promote an active and visible policy of mainstreaming a gender perspective in all policies and programs so that before decisions are taken, an analysis is made of the effects on women and men, respectively.

STRATEGIC OBJECTIVE G. 1.

⚘ *Take measures to ensure women's equal access to and full participation in power structures and decision-making*

Actions to be taken

190. By Governments:

(a) Commit themselves to establishing the goal of gender balance in governmental bodies and committees, as well as in public administrative entities, and in the judiciary, including, *inter alia*, setting specific targets and implementing measures to substantially increase the number of women with a view to achieving equal representation of women and men, if necessary through positive action, in all governmental and public administration positions;

(b) Take measures, including, where appropriate, in electoral systems that encourage political parties to integrate women in elective and non-elective public positions in the same proportion and at the same levels as men;

(c) Protect and promote the equal rights of women and men to engage in political activities and to freedom of association, including membership in political parties and trade unions;

(d) Review the differential impact of electoral systems on the political representation of women in elected bodies and consider, where appropriate, the adjustment or reform of those systems;

(e) Monitor and evaluate progress in the representation of women through the regular collection, analysis and dissemination of quantitative and qualitative data on women and men at all levels in various decisionmaking positions in the public and private sectors, and disseminate data on the number of women and men employed at various levels in Governments on a yearly basis; ensure that women and men have equal access to the full range of public appointments and set up mechanisms within governmental structures for monitoring progress in this field;

(f) Support non-governmental organizations and research institutes that conduct studies on women's participation in and impact on decisionmaking and the decision-making environment;

(g) Encourage greater involvement of indigenous women in decision-making at all levels;

(h) Encourage and, where appropriate, ensure that government- funded organizations adopt non-discriminatory policies and practices in order to increase the number and raise the position of women in their organizations;

(i) Recognize that shared work and parental responsibilities between women and men promote women's increased participation in public life, and take appropriate measures to achieve this, including measures to reconcile family and professional life;

(j) Aim at gender balance in the lists of national candidates nominated for election or appointment to United Nations bodies, specialized agencies and other autonomous organizations of the United Nations system, particularly for posts at the senior level.

191. By political parties:

(a) Consider examining party structures and procedures to remove all barriers that directly or indirectly discriminate against the participation of women;

(b) Consider developing initiatives that allow women to participate fully in all internal policy-making structures and appointive and electoral nominating processes;

(c) Consider incorporating gender issues in their political agenda, taking measures to ensure that women can participate in the leadership of political parties on an equal basis with men.

192. By Governments, national bodies, the private sector, political parties, trade unions, employers' organizations, research and academic institutions, subregional and regional bodies and non-governmental and international organizations:

(a) Take positive action to build a critical mass of women leaders, executives and managers in strategic decision-making positions;

(b) Create or strengthen, as appropriate, mechanisms to monitor women's access to senior levels of decision-making;

(c) Review the criteria for recruitment and appointment to advisory and decision-making bodies and promotion to senior positions to ensure that such criteria are relevant and do not discriminate against women;

(d) Encourage efforts by non-governmental organizations, trade unions and the private sector to achieve equality between women and men in their ranks, including equal participation in their decision-making bodies and in negotiations in all areas and at all levels;

(e) Develop communications strategies to promote public debate on the new roles of men and women in society, and in the family as defined in paragraph 29 above;

(f) Restructure recruitment and career-development programs to ensure that all women, especially young women, have equal access to managerial, entrepreneurial, technical and leadership training, including on-the-job training;

(g) Develop career advancement programs for women of all ages that include career planning, tracking, mentoring, coaching, training and retraining;

(h) Encourage and support the participation of women's non-governmental organizations in United Nations conferences and their preparatory processes;

(i) Aim at and support gender balance in the composition of delegations to the United Nations and other international forums.

193. By the United Nations:

(a) Implement existing and adopt new employment policies and measures in order to achieve overall gender equality, particularly at the Professional level and above, by the year 2000, with due regard to the importance of recruiting staff on as wide a geographical basis as possible, in conformity with Article 101, paragraph 3, of the Charter of the United Nations;

(b) Develop mechanisms to nominate women candidates for appointment to senior posts in the United Nations, the specialized agencies and other organizations and bodies of the United Nations system;

(c) Continue to collect and disseminate quantitative and qualitative data on women and men in decision-making and analyze their differential impact

on decision-making and monitor progress towards achieving the Secretary General's target of having women hold 50 per cent of managerial and decision-making positions by the year 2000.

194. By women's organizations, non-governmental organizations, trade unions, social partners, producers, and industrial and professional organizations:

(a) Build and strengthen solidarity among women through information, education and sensitization activities;

(b) Advocate at all levels to enable women to influence political, economic and social decisions, processes and systems, and work towards seeking accountability from elected representatives on their commitment to gender concerns;

(c) Establish, consistent with data protection legislation, databases on women and their qualification for use in appointing women to senior decision-making and advisory positions, for dissemination to Governments, regional and international organizations and private enterprise, political parties and other relevant bodies.

STRATEGIC OBJECTIVE G.2.

> *Increase women's capacity to participate in decision-making and leadership*

Actions to be taken

195. By Governments, national bodies, the private sector, political parties, trade unions, employers' organizations, subregional and regional bodies, non-governmental and international organizations and educational institutions:

(a) Provide leadership and self-esteem training to assist women and girls, particularly those with special needs, women with disabilities and women belonging to racial and ethnic minorities to strengthen their self-esteem and to encourage them to take decision-making positions;

(b) Have transparent criteria for decision-making positions and ensure that the selecting bodies have a gender-balanced composition;

(c) Create a system of mentoring for inexperienced women and, in particular, offer training, including training in leadership and decision making, public speaking and self-assertion, as well as in political campaigning;

(d) Provide gender-sensitive training for women and men to promote non discriminatory working relationships and respect for diversity in work and management styles;

(e) Develop mechanisms and training to encourage women to participate in the electoral process, political activities and other leadership areas.

Chapter IV. H

INSTITUTIONAL MECHANISMS FOR THE ADVANCEMENT OF WOMEN

196. National machineries for the advancement of women have been established in almost every Member State to, *inter alia*, design, promote the implementation of, execute, monitor, evaluate, advocate and mobilize support for policies that promote the advancement of women. National machineries are diverse in form and uneven in their effectiveness, and in some cases have declined. Often marginalized in national government structures, these mechanisms are frequently hampered by unclear mandates, lack of adequate staff, training, data and sufficient resources, and insufficient support from national political leadership.

197. At the regional and international levels, mechanisms and institutions to promote the advancement of women as an integral part of mainstream political, economic, social and cultural development, and of initiatives on development and human rights, encounter similar problems emanating from a lack of commitment at the highest levels.

198. Successive international conferences have underscored the need to take gender factors into account in policy and program planning. However, in many instances this has not been done.

199. Regional bodies concerned with the advancement of women have been strengthened, together with international machinery, such as the Commission on the Status of Women and the Committee on the Elimination of Discrimination against Women. However, the limited resources available continue to impede full implementation of their mandates.

200. Methodologies for conducting gender-based analysis in policies and programs and for dealing with the differential effects of policies on women and men have been developed in many organizations and are available for application but are often not being applied or are not being applied consistently.

201. A national machinery for the advancement of women is the central policy-coordinating unit inside government. Its main task is to support government-wide mainstreaming of a gender-equality per-

spective in all policy areas. The necessary conditions for an effective functioning of such national machineries include:

(a) Location at the highest possible level in the Government, falling under the responsibility of a Cabinet minister;

(b) Institutional mechanisms or processes that facilitate, as appropriate, decentralized planning, implementation and monitoring with a view to involving non-governmental organizations and community organizations from the grass-roots upwards;

(c) Sufficient resources in terms of budget and professional capacity;

(d) Opportunity to influence development of all government policies.

202. In addressing the issue of mechanisms for promoting the advancement of women, Governments and other actors should promote an active and visible policy of mainstreaming a gender perspective in all policies and programs so that, before decisions are taken, an analysis is made of the effects on women and men, respectively.

STRATEGIC OBJECTIVE H.1.

> ❧ *Create or strengthen national machineries and other governmental bodies*

Actions to be taken

203. By Governments:

(a) Ensure that responsibility for the advancement of women is vested in the highest possible level of government; in many cases, this could be at the level of a Cabinet minister;

(b) Based on a strong political commitment, create a national machinery, where it does not exist, and strengthen, as appropriate, existing national machineries, for the advancement of women at the highest possible level of government; it should have clearly defined mandates and authority; critical elements would be adequate resources and the ability and competence to influence policy and formulate and review legislation; among other things, it should perform policy analysis, undertake advocacy, communication, coordination and monitoring of implementation;

(c) Provide staff training in designing and analyzing data from a gender perspective;

(d) Establish procedures to allow the machinery to gather information on government-wide policy issues at an early stage and continuously use it in the policy development and review process within the Government;

(e) Report, on a regular basis, to legislative bodies on the progress of efforts, as appropriate, to mainstream gender concerns, taking into account the implementation of the PLATFORM FOR ACTION;

(f) Encourage and promote the active involvement of the broad and diverse range of institutional actors in the public, private and voluntary sectors to work for equality between women and men.

STRATEGIC OBJECTIVE H. 2.

✎ Integrate gender perspectives in legislation, public policies, programs and projects

Actions to be taken

204. By Governments:

(a) Seek to ensure that before policy decisions are taken, an analysis of their impact on women and men, respectively, is carried out;

(b) Regularly review national policies, programs and projects, as well as their implementation, evaluating the impact of employment and income policies in order to guarantee that women are direct beneficiaries of development and that their full contribution to development, both remunerated and unremunerated, is considered in economic policy and planning;

(c) Promote national strategies and aims on equality between women and men in order to eliminate obstacles to the exercise of women's rights and eradicate all forms of discrimination against women;

(d) Work with members of legislative bodies, as appropriate, to promote a gender perspective in all legislation and policies;

(e) Give all ministries the mandate to review policies and programs from a gender perspective and in the light of the PLATFORM FOR ACTION ; locate the responsibility for the implementation of that mandate at the highest possible level; establish and/or strengthen an inter-ministerial coordination structure to carry out this mandate, to monitor progress and to network with relevant machineries.

205. By national machinery:

(a) Facilitate the formulation and implementation of government policies on equality between women and men, develop appropriate strategies and methodologies, and promote coordination and cooperation within the central Government in order to ensure mainstreaming of a gender perspective in all policy-making processes;

(b) Promote and establish cooperative relationships with relevant branches of government, centers for women's studies and research, academic and educational institutions, the private sector, the media, non-governmental organizations, especially women's organizations, and all other actors of civil society;

(c) Undertake activities focusing on legal reform with regard, *inter alia*, to the family, conditions of employment, social security, income tax, equal opportunity in education, positive measures to promote the advancement of

women, and the perception of attitudes and a culture favorable to equality, as well as promote a gender perspective in legal policy and programming reforms;

(d) Promote the increased participation of women as both active agents and beneficiaries of the development process, which would result in an improvement in the quality of life for all;

(e) Establish direct links with national, regional and international bodies dealing with the advancement of women;

(f) Provide training and advisory assistance to government agencies in order to integrate a gender perspective in their policies and programs.

STRATEGIC OBJECTIVE H.3.

≫ *Generate and disseminate gender-disaggregated data and information for planning and evaluation*

Actions to be taken

206. By national, regional and international statistical services and relevant governmental and United Nations agencies, in cooperation with research and documentation organizations, in their respective areas of responsibility:

(a) Ensure that statistics related to individuals are collected, compiled, analyzed and presented by sex and age and reflect problems, issues and questions related to women and men in society;

(b) Collect, compile, analyze and present on a regular basis data disaggregated by age, sex, socio-economic and other relevant indicators, including number of dependents, for utilization in policy and program planning and implementation;

(c) Involve centers for women's studies and research organizations in developing and testing appropriate indicators and research methodologies to strengthen gender analysis, as well as in monitoring and evaluating the implementation of the goals of the PLATFORM FOR ACTION ;

(d) Designate or appoint staff to strengthen gender-statistics programs and ensure coordination, monitoring and linkage to all fields of statistical work, and prepare output that integrates statistics from the various subject areas;

(e) Improve data collection on the full contribution of women and men to the economy, including their participation in the informal sector(s) ;

(f) Develop a more comprehensive knowledge of all forms of work and employment by:

(i) Improving data collection on the unremunerated work which is already included in the United Nations System of National Accounts, such as in agriculture, particularly subsistence agriculture, and other types of non market production activities;

(ii)Improving measurements that at present underestimate women's unemployment and underemployment in the labor market;

(iii)Developing methods, in the appropriate forums, for assessing the value, in quantitative terms, of unremunerated work that is outside national accounts, such as caring for dependents and preparing food, for possible reflection in satellite or other official accounts that may be produced separately from but are consistent with core national accounts, with a view to recognizing the economic contribution of women and making visible the unequal distribution of remunerated and unremunerated work between women and men;

(g) Develop an international classification of activities for time-use statistics that is sensitive to the differences between women and men in remunerated and unremunerated work, and collect data disaggregated by sex. At the national level, subject to national constraints:

(i) Conduct regular time-use studies to measure, in quantitative terms, unremunerated work, including recording those activities that are performed simultaneously with remunerated or other unremunerated activities;

(ii)Measure, in quantitative terms, unremunerated work that is outside national accounts and work to improve methods to assess and accurately reflect its value in satellite or other official accounts that are separate from but consistent with core national accounts;

(h) Improve concepts and methods of data collection on the measurement of poverty among women and men, including their access to resources;

(i) Strengthen vital statistical systems and incorporate gender analysis into publications and research; give priority to gender differences in research design and in data collection and analysis in order to improve data on morbidity; and improve data collection on access to health services, including access to comprehensive sexual and reproductive health services, maternal care and family planning, with special priority for adolescent mothers and for elder care;

(j) Develop improved gender-disaggregated and age-specific data on the victims and perpetrators of all forms of violence against women, such as domestic violence, sexual harassment, rape, incest and sexual abuse, and trafficking in women and girls, as well as on violence by agents of the State;

(k) Improve concepts and methods of data collection on the participation of women and men with disabilities, including their access to resources

207. By Governments:

(a) Ensure the regular production of a statistical publication on gender that presents and interprets topical data on women and men in a form suitable for a wide range of non-technical users;

(b) Ensure that producers and users of statistics in each country regularly review the adequacy of the official statistical system and its coverage of gender issues, and prepare a plan for needed improvements, where necessary;

(c) Develop and encourage the development of quantitative and qualitative studies by research organizations, trade unions, employers, the private sector and non-governmental organizations on the sharing of power and influence in society, including the number of women and men in senior decision-making positions in both the public and private sectors;

(d) Use more gender-sensitive data in the formulation of policy and implementation of programs and projects.

208. By the United Nations:

(a) Promote the development of methods to find better ways to collect, collate and analyze data that may relate to the human rights of women, including violence against women, for use by all relevant United Nations bodies;

(b) Promote the further development of statistical methods to improve data that relate to women in economic, social, cultural and political development;

(c) Prepare a new issue of *The World's Women* at regular five-year intervals and distribute it widely;

(d) Assist countries, upon request, in the development of gender policies and programs;

(e) Ensure that the relevant reports, data and publications of the Statistical Division of the United Nations Secretariat and the International Research and Training Institute for the Advancement of Women on progress at the national and international levels are transmitted to the Commission on the Status of Women in a regular and coordinated fashion.

209. By multilateral development institutions and bilateral donors: Encourage and support the development of national capacity in developing countries and in countries with economies in transition by providing resources and technical assistance so that countries can fully measure the work done by women and men, including both remunerated and unremunerated work, and, where appropriate, use satellite or other official accounts for unremunerated work.

Chapter IV. I

HUMAN RIGHTS OF WOMEN

210. Human rights and fundamental freedoms are the birthright of all human beings; their protection and promotion is the first responsibility of Governments.

211. The World Conference on Human Rights reaffirmed the solemn commitment of all States to fulfill their obligation to promote universal respect for, and observance and protection of, all human rights and fundamental freedoms for all, in accordance with the Charter of the United Nations, other instruments relating to human rights, and international law. The universal nature of these rights and freedoms is beyond question.

212. The promotion and protection of all human rights and fundamental freedoms must be considered as a priority objective of the United Nations, in accordance with its purposes and principles, in particular with the purpose of international cooperation. In the framework of these purposes and principles, the promotion and protection of all human rights is a legitimate concern of the international community. The international community must treat human rights globally, in a fair and equal manner, on the same footing, and with the same emphasis. The PLATFORM FOR ACTION reaffirms the importance of ensuring the universality, objectivity and non selectivity of the consideration of human rights issues.

213. The PLATFORM FOR ACTION reaffirms that all human rights - civil, cultural, economic, political and social, including the right to development - are universal, indivisible, interdependent and interrelated, as expressed in the Vienna Declaration and Program of Action adopted by the World Conference on Human Rights. The Conference reaffirmed that the human rights of women and the girl child are an inalienable, integral and indivisible part of universal human rights. The full and equal enjoyment of all human rights and fundamental freedoms by women and girls is a priority for Governments and the United Nations and is essential for the advancement of women.

214. Equal rights of men and women are explicitly mentioned in the Preamble to the Charter of the United Nations. All the major international human rights instruments include sex as one of the grounds upon which States may not discriminate.

215. Governments must not only refrain from violating the human rights of all women, but must work actively to promote and protect these rights. Recognition of the importance of the human rights of women is reflected in the fact that three quarters of the States Members of the United Nations have become parties to the Convention on the Elimination of All Forms of Discrimination against Women.

216. The World Conference on Human Rights reaffirmed clearly that the human rights of women throughout the life cycle are an inalienable, integral and indivisible part of universal human rights. The International Conference on Population and Development reaffirmed women's reproductive rights and the right to development. Both the Declaration of the Rights of the Child[31]and the Convention on the Rights of the Child[11] guarantee children's rights and uphold the principle of non-discrimination on the grounds of gender.

217. The gap between the existence of rights and their effective enjoyment derives from a lack of commitment by Governments to promoting and protecting those rights and the failure of Governments to inform women and men alike about them. The lack of appropriate recourse mechanisms at the national and international levels, and inadequate resources at both levels, compound the problem. In most countries, steps have been taken to reflect the rights guaranteed by the Convention on the Elimination of All Forms of Discrimination against Women in national law. A number of countries have established mechanisms to strengthen women's ability to exercise their rights.

218. In order to protect the human rights of women, it is necessary to avoid, as far as possible, resorting to reservations and to ensure that no reservation is incompatible with the object and purpose of the Convention or is otherwise incompatible with international treaty law. Unless the human rights of women, as defined by international human rights instruments, are fully recognized and effectively protected, applied, implemented and enforced in national law as well as in national practice in family, civil, penal, labor and commercial codes and administrative rules and regulations, they will exist in name only.

219. In those countries that have not yet become parties to the Convention on the Elimination of All Forms of Discrimination against Women and other international human rights instruments, or where reservations that are incompatible with the object or purpose of the Convention have been entered, or where national laws have not yet been revised to implement international norms and standards, women's de jure equality is not yet secured. Women's full enjoyment of equal rights is undermined by the discrepancies between

some national legislation and international law and international instruments on human rights. Overly complex administrative procedures, lack of awareness within the judicial process and inadequate monitoring of the violation of the human rights of all women, coupled with the underrepresentation of women in justice systems, insufficient information on existing rights and persistent attitudes and practices perpetuate women's de facto inequality. De facto inequality is also perpetuated by the lack of enforcement of, *inter alia*, family, civil, penal, labor and commercial laws or codes, or administrative rules and regulations intended to ensure women's full enjoyment of human rights and fundamental freedoms.

220. Every person should be entitled to participate in, contribute to and enjoy cultural, economic, political and social development. In many cases women and girls suffer discrimination in the allocation of economic and social resources. This directly violates their economic, social and cultural rights.

221. The human rights of all women and the girl child must form an integral part of United Nations human rights activities. Intensified efforts are needed to integrate the equal status and the human rights of all women and girls into the mainstream of United Nations system-wide activities and to address these issues regularly and systematically throughout relevant bodies and mechanisms. This requires, *inter alia*, improved cooperation and coordination between the Commission on the Status of Women, the United Nations High Commissioner for Human Rights, the Commission on Human Rights, including its special and thematic rapporteurs, independent experts, working groups and its Subcommission on Prevention of Discrimination and Protection of Minorities, the Commission on Sustainable Development, the Commission for Social Development, the Commission on Crime Prevention and Criminal Justice, and the Committee on the Elimination of Discrimination against Women and other human rights treaty bodies, and all relevant entities of the United Nations system, including the specialized agencies. Cooperation is also needed to strengthen, rationalize and streamline the United Nations human rights system and to promote its effectiveness and efficiency, taking into account the need to avoid unnecessary duplication and overlapping of mandates and tasks.

222. If the goal of full realization of human rights for all is to be achieved, international human rights instruments must be applied in such a way as to take more clearly into consideration the systematic and systemic nature of discrimination against women that gender analysis has clearly indicated.

223. Bearing in mind the Program of Action of the International Conference on Population and Development[14] and the Vienna

Declaration and Program of Action[2] adopted by the World Conference on Human Rights, the Fourth World Conference on Women reaffirms that reproductive rights rest on the recognition of the basic right of all couples and individuals to decide freely and responsibly the number, spacing and timing of their children and to have the information and means to do so, and the right to attain the highest standard of sexual and reproductive health. It also includes their right to make decisions concerning reproduction free of discrimination, coercion and violence, as expressed in human rights documents.

224. Violence against women both violates and impairs or nullifies the enjoyment by women of human rights and fundamental freedoms. Taking into account the *Declaration on the Elimination of Violence against Women* and the work of Special Rapporteurs, gender-based violence, such as battering and other domestic violence, sexual abuse, sexual slavery and exploitation, and international trafficking in women and children, forced prostitution and sexual harassment, as well as violence against women, resulting from cultural prejudice, racism and racial discrimination, xenophobia, pornography, ethnic cleansing, armed conflict, foreign occupation, religious and anti-religious extremism and terrorism are incompatible with the dignity and the worth of the human person and must be combated and eliminated. Any harmful aspect of certain traditional, customary or modern practices that violates the rights of women should be prohibited and eliminated. Governments should take urgent action to combat and eliminate all forms of violence against women in private and public life, whether perpetrated or tolerated by the State or private persons.

225. Many women face additional barriers to the enjoyment of their human rights because of such factors as their race, language, ethnicity, culture, religion, disability or socio-economic class or because they are indigenous people, migrants, including women migrant workers, displaced women or refugees. They may also be disadvantaged and marginalized by a general lack of knowledge and recognition of their human rights as well as by the obstacles they meet in gaining access to information and recourse mechanisms in cases of violation of their rights.

226. The factors that cause the flight of refugee women, other displaced women in need of international protection and internally displaced women may be different from those affecting men. These women continue to be vulnerable to abuses of their human rights during and after their flight.

227. While women are increasingly using the legal system to exercise their rights, in many countries lack of awareness of the existence of

these rights is an obstacle that prevents women from fully enjoying their human rights and attaining equality. Experience in many countries has shown that women can be empowered and motivated to assert their rights, regardless of their level of education or socio-economic status. Legal literacy programs and media strategies have been effective in helping women to understand the link between their rights and other aspects of their lives and in demonstrating that cost-effective initiatives can be undertaken to help women obtain those rights. Provision of human rights education is essential for promoting an understanding of the human rights of women, including knowledge of recourse mechanisms to redress violations of their rights. It is necessary for all individuals, especially women in vulnerable circumstances, to have full knowledge of their rights and access to legal recourse against violations of their rights.

228. Women engaged in the defense of human rights must be protected. Governments have a duty to guarantee the full enjoyment of all rights set out in the *Universal Declaration of Human Rights, the International Covenant on Civil and Political Rights* and *the International Covenant on Economic, Social and Cultural Rights* by women working peacefully in a personal or organizational capacity for the promotion and protection of human rights. Non-governmental organizations, women's organizations and feminist groups have played a catalytic role in the promotion of the human rights of women through grass-roots activities, networking and advocacy and need encouragement, support and access to information from Governments in order to carry out these activities.

229. In addressing the enjoyment of human rights, Governments and other actors should promote an active and visible policy of mainstreaming a gender perspective in all policies and programs so that, before decisions are taken, an analysis is made of the effects on women and men, respectively.

STRATEGIC OBJECTIVE I.1.

> ✎ *Promote and protect the human rights of women, through the full implementation of all human rights instruments, especially the Convention on the Elimination of All Forms of Discrimination against Women*

Actions to be taken

230. By Governments:

   (a) Work actively towards ratification of or accession to and implement international and regional human rights treaties;

(*b*) Ratify and accede to and ensure implementation of the Convention on the Elimination of All Forms of Discrimination against Women so that universal ratification of the Convention can be achieved by the year 2000;

(*c*) Limit the extent of any reservations to the Convention on the Elimination of All Forms of Discrimination against Women; formulate any such reservations as precisely and as narrowly as possible; ensure that no reservations are incompatible with the object and purpose of the Convention or otherwise incompatible with international treaty law and regularly review them with a view to withdrawing them; and withdraw reservations that are contrary to the object and purpose of the Convention on the Elimination of All Forms of Discrimination against Women or which are otherwise incompatible with international treaty law;

(*d*) Consider drawing up national action plans identifying steps to improve the promotion and protection of human rights, including the human rights of women, as recommended by the World Conference on Human Rights;

(*e*) Create or strengthen independent national institutions for the protection and promotion of these rights, including the human rights of women, as recommended by the World Conference on Human Rights;

(*f*) Develop a comprehensive human rights education program to raise awareness among women of their human rights and raise awareness among others of the human rights of women;

(*g*) If they are States parties, implement the Convention by reviewing all national laws, policies, practices and procedures to ensure that they meet the obligations set out in the Convention; all States should undertake a review of all national laws, policies, practices and procedures to ensure that they meet international human rights obligations in this matter;

(*h*) Include gender aspects in reporting under all other human rights conventions and instruments, including ILO conventions, to ensure analysis and review of the human rights of women;

(*i*) Report on schedule to the Committee on the Elimination of Discrimination against Women regarding the implementation of the Convention, following fully the guidelines established by the Committee and involving non-governmental organizations, where appropriate, or taking into account their contributions in the preparation of the report;

(*j*) Enable the Committee on the Elimination of Discrimination against Women fully to discharge its mandate by allowing for adequate meeting time through broad ratification of the revision adopted by the States parties to the Convention on the Elimination of All Forms of Discrimination against Women on 22 May 1995 relative to article 20, paragraph 1,[32] and by promoting efficient working methods;

(*k*) Support the process initiated by the Commission on the Status of Women with a view to elaborating a draft optional protocol to the Convention on the Elimination of All Forms of Discrimination against Women that could enter into force as soon as possible on a right of petition procedure, taking into consideration the Secretary-General's report on the optional protocol, including those views related to its feasibility;

(*l*) Take urgent measures to achieve universal ratification of or accession to the Convention on the Rights of the Child before the end of 1995 and full implementation of the Convention in order to ensure equal rights for girls and boys; those that have not already done so are urged to become parties in order to realize universal implementation of the Convention on the Rights of the Child by the year 2000;

(*m*) Address the acute problems of children, *inter alia*, by supporting efforts in the context of the United Nations system aimed at adopting efficient international measures for the prevention and eradication of female infanticide, harmful child labor, the sale of children and their organs, child prostitution, child pornography and other forms of sexual abuse and consider contributing to the drafting of an optional protocol to the Convention on the Rights of the Child;

(*n*) Strengthen the implementation of all relevant human rights instruments in order to combat and eliminate, including through international cooperation, organized and other forms of trafficking in women and children, including trafficking for the purposes of sexual exploitation, pornography, prostitution and sex tourism, and provide legal and social services to the victims; this should include provisions for international cooperation to prosecute and punish those responsible for organized exploitation of women and children;

(*o*) Taking into account the need to ensure full respect for the human rights of indigenous women, consider a declaration on the rights of indigenous people for adoption by the General Assembly within the International Decade of the World's Indigenous People and encourage the participation of indigenous women in the working group elaborating the draft declaration, in accordance with the provisions for the participation of organizations of indigenous people.

231. By relevant organs, bodies and agencies of the United Nations system, all human rights bodies of the United Nations system, as well as the United Nations High Commissioner for Human Rights and the United Nations High Commissioner for Refugees, while promoting greater efficiency and effectiveness through better coordination of the various bodies, mechanisms and procedures, taking into account the need to avoid unnecessary duplication and overlapping of their mandates and tasks:

(*a*) Give full, equal and sustained attention to the human rights of women in the exercise of their respective mandates to promote universal respect for and protection of all human rights - civil, cultural, economic, political and social rights, including the right to development;

(b) Ensure the implementation of the recommendations of the World Conference on Human Rights for the full integration and mainstreaming of the human rights of women;

(c) Develop a comprehensive policy program for mainstreaming the human rights of women throughout the United Nations system, including activities with regard to advisory services, technical assistance, reporting methodology, gender-impact assessments, coordination, public information and human rights education, and play an active role in the implementation of the program;

(d) Ensure the integration and full participation of women as both agents and beneficiaries in the development process and reiterate the objectives established for global action for women towards sustainable and equitable development set forth in the Rio Declaration on Environment and Development;[18]

(e) Include information on gender-based human rights violations in their activities and integrate the findings into all of their programs and activities;

(f) Ensure that there is collaboration and coordination of the work of all human rights bodies and mechanisms to ensure that the human rights of women are respected;

(g) Strengthen cooperation and coordination between the Commission on the Status of Women, the Commission on Human Rights, the Commission for Social Development, the Commission on Sustainable Development, the Commission on Crime Prevention and Criminal Justice, the United Nations human rights treaty monitoring bodies, including the Committee on the Elimination of Discrimination against Women, and the United Nations Development Fund for Women, the International Research and Training Institute for the Advancement of Women, the United Nations Development Program, the United Nations Children's Fund and other organizations of the United Nations system, acting within their mandates, in the promotion of the human rights of women, and improve cooperation between the Division for the Advancement of Women and the Center for Human Rights;

(h) Establish effective cooperation between the United Nations High Commissioner for Human Rights and the United Nations High Commissioner for Refugees and other relevant bodies, within their respective mandates, taking into account the close link between massive violations of human rights, especially in the form of genocide, ethnic cleansing, systematic rape of women in war situations and refugee flows and other displacements, and the fact that refugee, displaced and returnee women may be subject to particular human rights abuse;

(i) Encourage incorporation of a gender perspective in national programs of action and in human rights and national institutions, within the context of human rights advisory services programs;

(j) Provide training in the human rights of women for all United Nations personnel and officials, especially those in human rights and humanitarian relief activities, and promote their understanding of the human rights of women so that they recognize and deal with violations of the human rights of women and can fully take into account the gender aspect of their work;

(k) In reviewing the implementation of the plan of action for the United Nations Decade for Human Rights Education(1995-2004), take into account the results of the Fourth World Conference on Women.

STRATEGIC OBJECTIVE I. 2.

> ✎ *Ensure equality and non-discrimination under the law and in practice*

Actions to be taken

232. By Governments:

(a) Give priority to promoting and protecting the full and equal enjoyment by women and men of all human rights and fundamental freedoms without distinction of any kind as to race, color, sex, language, religion, political or other opinions, national or social origins, property, birth or other status;

(b) Provide constitutional guarantees and/or enact appropriate legislation to prohibit discrimination on the basis of sex for all women and girls of all ages and assure women of all ages equal rights and their full enjoyment;

(c) Embody the principle of the equality of men and women in their legislation and ensure, through law and other appropriate means, the practical realization of this principle;

(d) Review national laws, including customary laws and legal practices in the areas of family, civil, penal, labor and commercial law in order to ensure the implementation of the principles and procedures of all relevant international human rights instruments by means of national legislation, revoke any remaining laws that discriminate on the basis of sex and remove gender bias in the administration of justice;

(e) Strengthen and encourage the development of programs to protect the human rights of women in the national institutions on human rights that carry out programs, such as human rights commissions or ombudspersons, according them appropriate status, resources and access to the Government to assist individuals, in particular women, and ensure that these institutions pay adequate attention to problems involving the violation of the human rights of women;

(f) Take action to ensure that the human rights of women, including the rights referred to in paragraphs 94 to 96 above, are fully respected and protected;

(g) Take urgent action to combat and eliminate violence against women, which is a human rights violation, resulting from harmful traditional or customary practices, cultural prejudices and extremism;

(h) Prohibit female genital mutilation wherever it exists and give vigorous support to efforts among non-governmental and community organizations and religious institutions to eliminate such practices;

(i) Provide gender-sensitive human rights education and training to public officials, including, *inter alia*, police and military personnel, corrections officers, health and medical personnel, and social workers, including people who deal with migration and refugee issues, and teachers at all levels of the educational system, and make available such education and training also to the judiciary and members of parliament in order to enable them to better exercise their public responsibilities;

(j) Promote the equal right of women to be members of trade unions and other professional and social organizations;

(k) Establish effective mechanisms for investigating violations of the human rights of women perpetrated by any public official and take the necessary punitive legal measures in accordance with national laws;

(l) Review and amend criminal laws and procedures, as necessary, to eliminate any discrimination against women in order to ensure that criminal law and procedures guarantee women effective protection against, and prosecution of, crimes directed at or disproportionately affecting women, regardless of the relationship between the perpetrator and the victim, and ensure that women defendants, victims and/or witnesses are not revictimized or discriminated against in the investigation and prosecution of crimes;

(m) Ensure that women have the same right as men to be judges, advocates or other officers of the court, as well as police officers and prison and detention officers, among other things;

(n) Strengthen existing or establish readily available and free or affordable alternative administrative mechanisms and legal aid programs to assist disadvantaged women seeking redress for violations of their rights;

(o) Ensure that all women and non-governmental organizations and their members in the field of protection and promotion of all human rights civil, cultural, economic, political and social rights, including the right to development - enjoy fully all human rights and freedoms in accordance with the Universal Declaration of Human Rights and all other human rights instruments and the protection of national laws;

(p) Strengthen and encourage the implementation of the recommendations contained in the Standard Rules on the Equalization of Opportunities for Persons with Disabilities,[30] paying special attention to ensure non discrimination and equal enjoyment of all human rights and fundamental freedoms by women and girls with disabilities, including their access to information and services in the field of violence against women, as well as

their active participation in and economic contribution to all aspects of society;

(q) Encourage the development of gender-sensitive human rights programs.

STRATEGIC OBJECTIVE I. 3.

❧ *Achieve legal literacy*

Actions to be taken

233. By Governments and non-governmental organizations, the United Nations and other international organizations, as appropriate:

(a) Translate, whenever possible, into local and indigenous languages and into alternative formats appropriate for persons with disabilities and persons at lower levels of literacy, publicize and disseminate laws and information relating to the equal status and human rights of all women, including the Universal Declaration of Human Rights, the International Covenant on Civil and Political Rights, the International Covenant on Economic, Social and Cultural Rights, the Convention on the Elimination of All Forms of Discrimination against Women, the International Convention on the Elimination of All Forms of Racial Discrimination,[33] the Convention on the Rights of the Child, the Convention against Torture and Other Cruel, Inhuman or Degrading Treatment or Punishment, the Declaration on the Right to Development[34] and the Declaration on the Elimination of Violence against Women, as well as the outcomes of relevant United Nations conferences and summits and national reports to the Committee on the Elimination of Discrimination against Women;

(b) Publicize and disseminate such information in easily understandable formats and alternative formats appropriate for persons with disabilities, and persons at low levels of literacy;

(c) Disseminate information on national legislation and its impact on women, including easily accessible guidelines on how to use a justice system to exercise one's rights;

(d) Include information about international and regional instruments and standards in their public information and human rights education activities and in adult education and training programs, particularly for groups such as the military, the police and other law enforcement personnel, the judiciary, and legal and health professionals to ensure that human rights are effectively protected;

(e) Make widely available and fully publicize information on the existence of national, regional and international mechanisms for seeking redress when the human rights of women are violated;

(f) Encourage, coordinate and cooperate with local and regional women's groups, relevant non-governmental organizations, educators and the media, to implement programs in human rights education to make women aware of their human rights;

(g) Promote education on the human and legal rights of women in school curricula at all levels of education and undertake public campaigns, including in the most widely used languages of the country, on the equality of women and men in public and private life, including their rights within the family and relevant human rights instruments under national and international law;

(h) Promote education in all countries in human rights and international humanitarian law for members of the national security and armed forces, including those assigned to United Nations peace-keeping operations, on a routine and continuing basis, reminding them and sensitizing them to the fact that they should respect the rights of women at all times, both on and off duty, giving special attention to the rules on the protection of women and children and to the protection of human rights in situations of armed conflict;

(i) Take appropriate measures to ensure that refugee and displaced women, migrant women and women migrant workers are made aware of their human rights and of the recourse mechanisms available to them.

Chapter IV. J

WOMEN AND THE MEDIA

234. During the past decade, advances in information technology have facilitated a global communications network that transcends national boundaries and has an impact on public policy, private attitudes and behaviour, especially of children and young adults. Everywhere the potential exists for the media to make a far greater contribution to the advancement of women.

235. More women are involved in careers in the communications sector, but few have attained positions at the decision-making level or serve on governing boards and bodies that influence media policy. The lack of gender sensitivity in the media is evidenced by the failure to eliminate the gender-based stereotyping that can be found in public and private local, national and international media organizations.

236. The continued projection of negative and degrading images of women in media communications - electronic, print, visual and audio - must be changed. Print and electronic media in most countries do not provide a balanced picture of women's diverse lives and contributions to society in a changing world. In addition, violent and degrading or pornographic media products are also negatively affecting women and their participation in society. Programming that reinforces women's traditional roles can be equally limiting. The world-wide trend towards consumerism has created a climate in which advertisements and commercial messages often portray women primarily as consumers and target girls and women of all ages inappropriately.

237. Women should be empowered by enhancing their skills, knowledge and access to information technology. This will strengthen their ability to combat negative portrayals of women internationally and to challenge instances of abuse of the power of an increasingly important industry. Selfregulatory mechanisms for the media need to be created and strengthened and approaches developed to eliminate genderbiased programming. Most women, especially in developing countries, are not able to access effectively the expanding electronic information highways and therefore cannot establish networks that will provide them with alternative sources of information. Women therefore need to be involved in decision making re-

garding the development of the new technologies in order to participate fully in their growth and impact.

238. In addressing the issue of the mobilization of the media, Governments and other actors should promote an active and visible policy of mainstreaming a gender perspective in policies and programmes.

STRATEGIC OBJECTIVE J. 1.

> ☞ *Increase the participation and access of women to expression and decision- making in and through the media and new technologies of communication*

Actions to be taken

239. By Governments:

(a) Support women's education, training and employment to promote and ensure women's equal access to all areas and levels of the media;

(b) Support research into all aspects of women and the media so as to define areas needing attention and action and review existing media policies with a view to integrating a gender perspective;

(c) Promote women's full and equal participation in the media, including management, programming, education, training and research;

(d) Aim at gender balance in the appointment of women and men to all advisory, management, regulatory or monitoring bodies, including those connected to the private and State or public media;

(e) Encourage, to the extent consistent with freedom of expression, these bodies to increase the number of programmes for and by women to see to it that women's needs and concerns are properly addressed;

(f) Encourage and recognize women's media networks, including electronic networks and other new technologies of communication, as a means for the dissemination of information and the exchange of views, including at the international level, and support women's groups active in all media work and systems of communications to that end;

(g) Encourage and provide the means or incentives for the creative use of programmes in the national media for the dissemination of information on various cultural forms of indigenous people and the development of social and educational issues in this regard within the framework of national law;

(h) Guarantee the freedom of the media and its subsequent protection within the framework of national law and encourage, consistent with freedom of expression, the positive involvement of the media in development and social issues.

240. By national and international media systems:

Develop, consistent with freedom of expression, regulatory mechanisms, including voluntary ones, that promote balanced and diverse portrayals of women by the media and international communication systems and that promote increased participation by women and men in production and decision-making.

241. By Governments, as appropriate, or national machinery for the advancement of women:

(a) Encourage the development of educational and training programmes for women in order to produce information for the mass media, including funding of experimental efforts, and the use of the new technologies of communication, cybernetics space and satellite, whether public or private;

(b) Encourage the use of communication systems, including new technologies, as a means of strengthening women's participation in democratic processes;

(c) Facilitate the compilation of a directory of women media experts;

(d) Encourage the participation of women in the development of professional guidelines and codes of conduct or other appropriate self regulatory mechanisms to promote balanced and non-stereotyped portrayals of women by the media.

242. By non-governmental organizations and media professional associations:

(a) Encourage the establishment of media watch groups that can monitor the media and consult with the media to ensure that women's needs and concerns are properly reflected;

(b) Train women to make greater use of information technology for communication and the media, including at the international level;

(c) Create networks among and develop information programmes for non governmental organizations, women's organizations and professional media organizations in order to recognize the specific needs of women in the media, and facilitate the increased participation of women in communication, in particular at the international level, in support of South-South and North-South dialogue among and between these organizations, *inter alia*, to promote the human rights of women and equality between women and men;

(d) Encourage the media industry and education and media training institutions to develop, in appropriate languages, traditional, indigenous and other ethnic forms of media, such as story-telling, drama, poetry and song, reflecting their cultures, and utilize these forms of communication to disseminate information on development and social issues.

STRATEGIC OBJECTIVE J.2.

༈ *Promote a balanced and non-stereotyped portrayal of women in the media*

Actions to be taken

243. By Governments and international organizations, to the extent consistent with freedom of expression:

   (a) Promote research and implementation of a strategy of information, education and communication aimed at promoting a balanced portrayal of women and girls and their multiple roles;

   (b) Encourage the media and advertising agencies to develop specific programmes to raise awareness of the PLATFORM FOR ACTION;

   (c) Encourage gender-sensitive training for media professionals, including media owners and managers, to encourage the creation and use of non stereotyped, balanced and diverse images of women in the media;

   (d) Encourage the media to refrain from presenting women as inferior beings and exploiting them as sexual objects and commodities, rather than presenting them as creative human beings, key actors and contributors to and beneficiaries of the process of development;

   (e) Promote the concept that the sexist stereotypes displayed in the media are gender discriminatory, degrading in nature and offensive;

   (f) Take effective measures or institute such measures, including appropriate legislation against pornography and the projection of violence against women and children in the media.

244. By the mass media and advertising organizations:

   (a) Develop, consistent with freedom of expression, professional guidelines and codes of conduct and other forms of self-regulation to promote the presentation of non-stereotyped images of women;

   (b) Establish, consistent with freedom of expression, professional guidelines and codes of conduct that address violent, degrading or pornographic materials concerning women in the media, including advertising;

   (c) Develop a gender perspective on all issues of concern to communities, consumers and civil society;

   (d) Increase women's participation in decision-making at all levels of the media.

245. By the media, non-governmental organizations and the private sector, in collaboration, as appropriate, with national machinery for the advancement of women:

   (a) Promote the equal sharing of family responsibilities through media campaigns that emphasize gender equality and non-stereotyped gender roles of women and men within the family and that disseminate information aimed

at eliminating spousal and child abuse and all forms of violence against women, including domestic violence;

(b) Produce and/or disseminate media materials on women leaders, *inter alia*, as leaders who bring to their positions of leadership many different life experiences, including but not limited to their experiences in balancing work and family responsibilities, as mothers, as professionals, as managers and as entrepreneurs, to provide role models, particularly to young women;

(c) Promote extensive campaigns, making use of public and private educational programmes, to disseminate information about and increase awareness of the human rights of women;

(d) Support the development of and finance, as appropriate, alternative media and the use of all means of communication to disseminate information to and about women and their concerns;

(e) Develop approaches and train experts to apply gender analysis with regard to media programmes.

Chapter IV. K

WOMEN AND THE ENVIRONMENT

246. Human beings are at the center of concern for sustainable development. They are entitled to a healthy and productive life in harmony with nature. Women have an essential role to play in the development of sustainable and ecologically sound consumption and production patterns and approaches to natural resource management, as was recognized at the United Nations Conference on Environment and Development and the International Conference on Population and Development and reflected throughout Agenda 21. Awareness of resource depletion, the degradation of natural systems and the dangers of polluting substances has increased markedly in the past decade. These worsening conditions are destroying fragile ecosystems and displacing communities, especially women, from productive activities and are an increasing threat to a safe and healthy environment. Poverty and environmental degradation are closely interrelated. While poverty results in certain kinds of environmental stress, the major cause of the continued deterioration of the global environment is the unsustainable pattern of consumption and production, particularly in industrialized countries, which is a matter of grave concern, aggravating poverty and imbalances. Rising sea levels as a result of global warming cause a grave and immediate threat to people living in island countries and coastal areas. The use of ozone depleting substances, such as products with chlorofluorocarbons, halons and methyl bromides(from which plastics and foams are made), are severely affecting the atmosphere, thus allowing excessive levels of harmful ultraviolet rays to reach the Earth's surface. This has severe effects on people's health such as higher rates of skin cancer, eye damage and weakened immune systems. It also has severe effects on the environment, including harm to crops and ocean life.

247. All States and all people shall cooperate in the essential task of eradicating poverty as an indispensable requirement for sustainable development, in order to decrease the disparities in standards of living and better meet the needs of the majority of the people of the world. Hurricanes, typhoons and other natural disasters and, in addition, the destruction of resources, violence, displacements and

other effects associated with war, armed and other conflicts, the use and testing of nuclear weaponry, and foreign occupation can also contribute to environmental degradation. The deterioration of natural resources displaces communities, especially women, from income-generating activities while greatly adding to unremunerated work. In both urban and rural areas, environmental degradation results in negative effects on the health, well being and quality of life of the population at large, especially girls and women of all ages. Particular attention and recognition should be given to the role and special situation of women living in rural areas and those working in the agricultural sector, where access to training, land, natural and productive resources, credit, development programs and cooperative structures can help them increase their participation in sustainable development. Environmental risks in the home and workplace may have a disproportionate impact on women's health because of women's different susceptibilities to the toxic effects of various chemicals. These risks to women's health are particularly high in urban areas, as well as in low income areas where there is a high concentration of polluting industrial facilities.

248. Through their management and use of natural resources, women provide sustenance to their families and communities. As consumers and producers, caretakers of their families and educators, women play an important role in promoting sustainable development through their concern for the quality and sustainability of life for present and future generations. Governments have expressed their commitment to creating a new development paradigm that integrates environmental sustainability with gender equality and justice within and between generations as contained in chapter 24 of Agenda 21.[19]

249. Women remain largely absent at all levels of policy formulation and decision-making in natural resource and environmental management, conservation, protection and rehabilitation, and their experience and skills in advocacy for and monitoring of proper natural resource management too often remain marginalized in policy-making and decision-making bodies, as well as in educational institutions and environment-related agencies at the managerial level. Women are rarely trained as professional natural resource managers with policy-making capacities, such as land-use planners, agriculturalists, foresters, marine scientists and environmental lawyers. Even in cases where women are trained as professional natural resource managers, they are often underrepresented in formal institutions with policy-making capacities at the national, regional and international levels. Often women are not equal participants in the management of financial and corporate institutions whose decision-

making most significantly affects environmental quality. Furthermore, there are institutional weaknesses in coordination between women's non-governmental organizations and national institutions dealing with environmental issues, despite the recent rapid growth and visibility of women's non-governmental organizations working on these issues at all levels.

250. Women have often played leadership roles or taken the lead in promoting an environmental ethic, reducing resource use, and re-using and recycling resources to minimize waste and excessive consumption. Women can have a particularly powerful role in influencing sustainable consumption decisions. In addition, women's contributions to environmental management, including through grass-roots and youth campaigns to protect the environment, have often taken place at the local level, where decentralized action on environmental issues is most needed and decisive. Women, especially indigenous women, have particular knowledge of ecological linkages and fragile ecosystem management. Women in many communities provide the main labor force for subsistence production, including production of seafood; hence, their role is crucial to the provision of food and nutrition, the enhancement of the subsistence and informal sectors and the preservation of the environment. In certain regions, women are generally the most stable members of the community, as men often pursue work in distant locations, leaving women to safeguard the natural environment and ensure adequate and sustainable resource allocation within the household and the community.

251. The strategic actions needed for sound environmental management require a holistic, multidisciplinary and intersectoral approach. Women's participation and leadership are essential to every aspect of that approach. The recent United Nations global conferences on development, as well as regional preparatory conferences for the Fourth World Conference on Women, have all acknowledged that sustainable development policies that do not involve women and men alike will not succeed in the long run. They have called for the effective participation of women in the generation of knowledge and environmental education in decision-making and management at all levels. Women's experiences and contributions to an ecologically sound environment must therefore be central to the agenda for the twenty-first century. Sustainable development will be an elusive goal unless women's contribution to environmental management is recognized and supported.

252. In addressing the lack of adequate recognition and support for women's contribution to conservation and management of natural resources and safeguarding the environment, Governments and

other actors should   promote an active and visible policy of mainstreaming a gender perspective in all policies and programs, including, as appropriate, an analysis of the effects on women and
men, respectively, before decisions are taken.

STRATEGIC OBJECTIVE K.1.

> *Involve women actively in environmental decision-making at*
> *all levels*

Actions to be taken

253. By Governments, at all levels, including municipal authorities, as
appropriate:

(a) Ensure opportunities for women, including indigenous women, to participate in environmental decision-making at all levels, including as managers, designers and planners, and as implementers and evaluators of environmental projects;

(b) Facilitate and increase women's access to information and education, including in the areas of science, technology and economics, thus enhancing
their knowledge, skills and opportunities for participation in environmental decisions;

(c) Encourage, subject to national legislation and consistent with the Convention on Biological Diversity,[35] the effective protection and use of the
knowledge, innovations and practices of women of indigenous and local
communities, including practices relating to traditional medicines, biodi-
versity and indigenous technologies, and endeavor to ensure that these are
respected, maintained, promoted and preserved in an ecologically sustainable manner, and promote their wider application with the approval and involvement of the holders of such knowledge; in addition, safeguard the existing intellectual property rights of these women as protected under national and international law; work actively, where necessary, to find additional ways and means for the effective protection and use of such knowledge, innovations and practices, subject to national legislation and consistent with the Convention on Biological Diversity and relevant international law, and encourage fair and equitable sharing of benefits arising from
the utilization of such knowledge, innovation and practices;

(d) Take appropriate measures to reduce risks to women from identified environmental hazards at home, at work and in other environments, including
appropriate application of clean technologies, taking into account the precautionary approach agreed to in the Rio Declaration on Environment and
Development;[18]

(e) Take measures to integrate a gender perspective in the design and implementation of, among other things, environmentally sound and sustainable

resource management mechanisms, production techniques and infrastructure development in rural and urban areas;

(f) Take measures to empower women as producers and consumers so that they can take effective environmental actions, along with men, in their homes, communities and workplaces;

(g) Promote the participation of local communities, particularly women, in identification of public service needs, spatial planning and the provision and design of urban infrastructure.

254. By Governments and international organizations and private sector institutions, as appropriate:

(a) Take gender impact into consideration in the work of the Commission on Sustainable Development and other appropriate United Nations bodies and in the activities of international financial institutions;

(b) Promote the involvement of women and the incorporation of a gender perspective in the design, approval and execution of projects funded under the Global Environment Facility and other appropriate United Nations organizations;

(c) Encourage the design of projects in the areas of concern to the Global Environment Facility that would benefit women and projects managed by women;

(d) Establish strategies and mechanisms to increase the proportion of women, particularly at grass-roots levels, involved as decision makers, planners, managers, scientists and technical advisers and as beneficiaries in the design, development and implementation of policies and programs for natural resource management and environmental protection and conservation;

(e) Encourage social, economic, political and scientific institutions to address environmental degradation and the resulting impact on women.

255. By non-governmental organizations and the private sector:

a) Assume advocacy of environmental and natural resource management issues of concern to women and provide information to contribute to resource mobilization for environmental protection and conservation;

(b) Facilitate the access of women agriculturists, fishers and pastoralists to knowledge, skills, marketing services and environmentally sound technologies to support and strengthen their crucial roles and their expertise in resource management and the conservation of biological diversity.

STRATEGIC OBJECTIVE K.2.

9 *Integrate gender concerns and perspectives in policies and programs for sustainable development*

Actions to be taken

256. By Governments:

(a) Integrate women, including indigenous women, their perspectives and knowledge, on an equal basis with men, in decision-making regarding sustainable resource management and the development of policies and programs for sustainable development, including in particular those designed to address and prevent environmental degradation of the land;

(b) Evaluate policies and programs in terms of environmental impact and women's equal access to and use of natural resources;

(c) Ensure adequate research to assess how and to what extent women are particularly susceptible or exposed to environmental degradation and hazards, including, as necessary, research and data collection on specific groups of women, particularly women with low income, indigenous women and women belonging to minorities;

(d) Integrate rural women's traditional knowledge and practices of sustainable resource use and management in the development of environmental management and extension programs;

(e) Integrate the results of gender-sensitive research into mainstream policies with a view to developing sustainable human settlements;

(f) Promote knowledge of and sponsor research on the role of women, particularly rural and indigenous women, in food gathering and production, soil conservation, irrigation, watershed management, sanitation, coastal zone and marine resource management, integrated pest management, land-use planning, forest conservation and community forestry, fisheries, natural disaster prevention, and new and renewable sources of energy, focusing particularly on indigenous women's knowledge and experience;

(g) Develop a strategy for change to eliminate all obstacles to women's full and equal participation in sustainable development and equal access to and control over resources;

(h) Promote the education of girls and women of all ages in science, technology, economics and other disciplines relating to the natural environment so that they can make informed choices and offer informed input in determining local economic, scientific and environmental priorities for the management and appropriate use of natural and local resources and ecosystems;

(i) Develop programs to involve female professionals and scientists, as well as technical, administrative and clerical workers, in environmental management, develop training programs for girls and women in these fields, expand opportunities for the hiring and promotion of women in these fields and implement special measures to advance women's expertise and participation in these activities;

(j) Identify and promote environmentally sound technologies that have been designed, developed and improved in consultation with women and that are appropriate to both women and men;

(k) Support the development of women's equal access to housing infrastructure, safe water, and sustainable and affordable energy technologies, such as wind, solar, biomass and other renewable sources, through participatory needs assessments, energy planning and policy formulation at the local and national levels;

(l) Ensure that clean water is available and accessible to all by the year 2000 and that environmental protection and conservation plans are designed and implemented to restore polluted water systems and rebuild damaged watersheds.

257. By international organizations, non-governmental organizations and private sector institutions:

(a) Involve women in the communication industries in raising awareness regarding environmental issues, especially on the environmental and health impacts of products, technologies and industry processes;

(b) Encourage consumers to use their purchasing power to promote the production of environmentally safe products and encourage investment in environmentally sound and productive agricultural, fisheries, commercial and industrial activities and technologies;

(c) Support women's consumer initiatives by promoting the marketing of organic food and recycling facilities, product information and product labeling, including labeling of toxic chemical and pesticide containers with language and symbols that are understood by consumers, regardless of age and level of literacy.

STRATEGIC OBJECTIVE K.3.

> ❧ *Strengthen or establish mechanisms at the national, regional and international levels to assess the impact of development and environmental policies on women*

Actions to be taken

258. By Governments, regional and international organizations and non governmental organizations, as appropriate:

(a) Provide technical assistance to women, particularly in developing countries, in the sectors of agriculture, fisheries, small enterprises, trade and industry to ensure the continuing promotion of human resource development and the development of environmentally sound technologies and of women's entrepreneurship;

(b) Develop gender-sensitive databases, information and monitoring systems and participatory action-oriented research, methodologies and policy analy-

ses, with the collaboration of academic institutions and local women researchers, on the following:

(i) Knowledge and experience on the part of women concerning the management and conservation of natural resources for incorporation in the databases and information systems for sustainable development;

(ii)The impact on women of environmental and natural resource degradation, deriving from, *inter alia*, unsustainable production and consumption patterns, drought, poor quality water, global warming, desertification, sea level rise, hazardous waste, natural disasters, toxic chemicals and pesticide residues, radioactive waste, armed conflicts and its consequences;

(iii)Analysis of the structural links between gender relations, environment and development, with special emphasis on particular sectors, such as agriculture, industry, fisheries, forestry, environmental health, biological diversity, climate, water resources and sanitation;

(iv)Measures to develop and include environmental, economic, cultural, social and gender-sensitive analyses as an essential step in the development and monitoring of programs and policies;

(v) Programs to create rural and urban training, research and resource centers that will disseminate environmentally sound technologies to women;

(c) Ensure the full compliance with relevant international obligations, including where relevant, the Basel Convention and other conventions relating to the transboundary movements of hazardous wastes(which include toxic wastes) and the Code of Practice of the International Atomic Energy Agency relating to the movement of radioactive waste; enact and enforce regulations for environmentally sound management related to safe storage and movements; consider taking action towards the prohibition of those movements that are unsafe and insecure; ensure the strict control and management of hazardous wastes and radioactive waste, in accordance with relevant international and regional obligations and eliminate the exportation of such wastes to countries that, individually or through international agreements, prohibit their importation;

(d) Promote coordination within and among institutions to implement the PLATFORM FOR ACTION and chapter 24 of Agenda 21 by, *inter alia*, requesting the Commission on Sustainable Development, through the Economic and Social Council, to seek input from the Commission on the Status of Women when reviewing the implementation of Agenda 21 with regard to women and the environment.

Chapter IV. L

THE GIRL CHILD

259. The Convention on the Rights of the Child recognizes that "States Parties shall respect and ensure the rights set forth in the present Convention to each child within their jurisdiction without discrimination of any kind, irrespective of the child's or his or her parent's or legal guardian's race, color, sex, language, religion, political or other opinion, national, ethnic or social origin, property, disability, birth or status" (art. 2, para. 1).[11] However, in many countries available indicators show that the girl child is discriminated against from the earliest stages of life, through her childhood and into adulthood. In some areas of the world, men outnumber women by 5 in every 100. The reasons for the discrepancy include, among other things, harmful attitudes and practices, such as female genital mutilation, son preference - which results in female infanticide and prenatal sex selection - early marriage, including child marriage, violence against women, sexual exploitation, sexual abuse, discrimination against girls in food allocation and other practices related to health and well-being. As a result, fewer girls than boys survive into adulthood.

260. Girls are often treated as inferior and are socialized to put themselves last, thus undermining their self-esteem. Discrimination and neglect in childhood can initiate a lifelong downward spiral of deprivation and exclusion from the social mainstream. Initiatives should be taken to prepare girls to participate actively, effectively and equally with boys at all levels of social, economic, political and cultural leadership.

261. Gender-biased educational processes, including curricula, educational materials and practices, teachers' attitudes and classroom interaction, reinforce existing gender inequalities.

262. Girls and adolescents may receive a variety of conflicting and confusing messages on their gender roles from their parents, teachers, peers and the media. Women and men need to work together with children and youth to break down persistent gender stereotypes, taking into account the rights of the child and the responsibilities, rights and duties of parents as stated in paragraph 267 below.

263. Although the number of educated children has grown in the past 20 years in some countries, boys have proportionately fared much better than girls. In 1990, 130 million children had no access to primary school; of these, 81 million were girls. This can be attributed to such factors as customary attitudes, child labor, early marriages, lack of funds and lack of adequate schooling facilities, teenage pregnancies and gender inequalities in society at large as well as in the family as defined in paragraph 29 above. In some countries the shortage of women teachers can inhibit the enrollment of girls. In many cases, girls start to undertake heavy domestic chores at a very early age and are expected to manage both educational and domestic responsibilities, often resulting in poor scholastic performance and an early drop-out from schooling.

264. The percentage of girls enrolled in secondary school remains significantly low in many countries. Girls are often not encouraged or given the opportunity to pursue scientific and technological training and education, which limits the knowledge they require for their daily lives and their employment opportunities.

265. Girls are less encouraged than boys to participate in and learn about the social, economic and political functioning of society, with the result that they are not offered the same opportunities as boys to take part in decision-making processes.

266. Existing discrimination against the girl child in her access to nutrition and physical and mental health services endangers her current and future health. An estimated 450 million adult women in developing countries are stunted as a result of childhood protein-energy malnutrition.

267. The International Conference on Population and Development recognized, in paragraph 7.3 of the Program of Action,[14] that "full attention should be given to the promotion of mutually respectful and equitable gender relations and particularly to meeting the educational and service needs of adolescents to enable them to deal in a positive and responsible way with their sexuality", taking into account the rights of the child to access to information, privacy, confidentiality, respect and informed consent, as well as the responsibilities, rights and duties of parents and legal guardians to provide, in a manner consistent with the evolving capacities of the child, appropriate direction and guidance in the exercise by the child of the rights recognized in the Convention on the Rights of the Child, and in conformity with the Convention on the Elimination of All Forms of Discrimination against Women. In all actions concerning children, the best interests of the child shall be a primary consideration. Support should be given to integral sexual education for young people with parental support and guidance that stresses the respon-

sibility of males for their own sexuality and fertility and that help them exercise their responsibilities.

268. More than 15 million girls aged 15 to 19 give birth each year. Motherhood at a very young age entails complications during pregnancy and delivery and a risk of maternal death that is much greater than average. The children of young mothers have higher levels of morbidity and mortality. Early child-bearing continues to be an impediment to improvements in the educational, economic and social status of women in all parts of the world. Overall, early marriage and early motherhood can severely curtail educational and employment opportunities and are likely to have a long-term adverse impact on their and their children's quality of life.

269. Sexual violence and sexually transmitted diseases, including HIV/AIDS, have a devastating effect on children's health, and girls are more vulnerable than boys to the consequences of unprotected and premature sexual relations. Girls often face pressures to engage in sexual activity. Due to such factors as their youth, social pressures, lack of protective laws, or failure to enforce laws, girls are more vulnerable to all kinds of violence, particularly sexual violence, including rape, sexual abuse, sexual exploitation, trafficking, possibly the sale of their organs and tissues, and forced labor.

270. The girl child with disabilities faces additional barriers and needs to be ensured non-discrimination and equal enjoyment of all human rights and fundamental freedoms in accordance with the Standard Rules on the Equalization of Opportunities for Persons with Disabilities.[30]

271. Some children are particularly vulnerable, especially the abandoned, homeless and displaced, street children, children in areas in conflict, and children who are discriminated against because they belong to an ethnic or racial minority group.

272. All barriers must therefore be eliminated to enable girls without exception to develop their full potential and skills through equal access to education and training, nutrition, physical and mental health care and related information.

273. In addressing issues concerning children and youth, Governments should promote an active and visible policy of mainstreaming a gender perspective into all policies and programs so that before decisions are taken, an analysis is made of the effects on girls and boys, respectively.

STRATEGIC OBJECTIVE L. 1.

❧ *Eliminate all forms of discrimination against the girl child*

Actions to be taken

274. By Governments:

(*a*) By States that have not signed or ratified the Convention on the Rights of the Child, take urgent measures towards signing and ratifying the Convention, bearing in mind the strong exhortation made at the World Conference on Human Rights to sign it before the end of 1995, and by States that have signed and ratified the Convention, ensure its full implementation through the adoption of all necessary legislative, administrative and other measures and by fostering an enabling environment that encourages full respect for the rights of children;

(*b*) Consistent with article 7 of the Convention on the Rights of the Child[11] take measures to ensure that a child is registered immediately after birth and has the right from birth to a name, the right to acquire a nationality and, as far as possible, the right to know and be cared for by his or her parents;

(*c*) Take steps to ensure that children receive appropriate financial support from their parents, by, among other measures, enforcing child support laws;

(*d*) Eliminate the injustice and obstacles in relation to inheritance faced by the girl child so that all children may enjoy their rights without discrimination, by, *inter alia*, enacting, as appropriate, and enforcing legislation that guarantees equal right to succession and ensures equal right to inherit, regardless of the sex of the child;

(*e*) Enact and strictly enforce laws to ensure that marriage is only entered into with the free and full consent of the intending spouses; in addition, enact and strictly enforce laws concerning the minimum legal age of consent and the minimum age for marriage and raise the minimum age for marriage where necessary;

(*f*) Develop and implement comprehensive policies, plans of action and programs for the survival, protection, development and advancement of the girl child to promote and protect the full enjoyment of her human rights and to ensure equal opportunities for girls; these plans should form an integral part of the total development process;

(*g*) Ensure the disaggregation by sex and age of all data related to children in the health, education and other sectors in order to include a gender perspective in planning, implementation and monitoring of such programs.

275. By Governments and international and non-governmental organizations:

(*a*) Disaggregate information and data on children by sex and age, undertake research on the situation of girls and integrate, as appropriate, the results in the formulation of policies, programs and decision-making for the advancement of the girl child;

(b) Generate social support for the enforcement of laws on the minimum legal age for marriage, in particular by providing educational opportunities for girls.

STRATEGIC OBJECTIVE L. 2.

> ❧ *Eliminate negative cultural attitudes and practices against girls*

Actions to be taken

276. By Governments:

(a) Encourage and support, as appropriate, non-governmental organizations and community-based organizations in their efforts to promote changes in negative attitudes and practices towards girls;

(b) Set up educational programs and develop teaching materials and textbooks that will sensitize and inform adults about the harmful effects of certain traditional or customary practices on girl children;

(c) Develop and adopt curricula, teaching materials and textbooks to improve the self-image, lives and work opportunities of girls, particularly in areas where women have traditionally been underrepresented, such as mathematics, science and technology;

(d) Take steps so that tradition and religion and their expressions are not a basis for discrimination against girls.

277. By Governments and, as appropriate, international and non governmental organizations:

(a) Promote an educational setting that eliminates all barriers that impede the schooling of married and/or pregnant girls and young mothers, including, as appropriate, affordable and physically accessible child-care facilities and parental education to encourage those who have responsibilities for the care of their children and siblings during their school years to return to, or continue with, and complete schooling;

(b) Encourage educational institutions and the media to adopt and project balanced and non-stereotyped images of girls and boys, and work to eliminate child pornography and degrading and violent portrayals of the girl child;

(c) Eliminate all forms of discrimination against the girl child and the root causes of son preference, which result in harmful and unethical practices such as prenatal sex selection and female infanticide; this is often compounded by the increasing use of technologies to determine fetal sex, resulting in abortion of female fetuses;

(d) Develop policies and programs, giving priority to formal and informal education programs that support girls and enable them to acquire knowledge, develop self-esteem and take responsibility for their own lives; and place special focus on programs to educate women and men, especially parents, on the importance of girls' physical and mental health and well being, including the elimination of discrimination against girls in food allo-

cation, early marriage, violence against girls, female genital mutilation, child prostitution, sexual abuse, rape and incest.

STRATEGIC OBJECTIVE L.3.

> Promote and protect the rights of the girl child and increase awareness of her needs and potential

---

Actions to be taken

278. By Governments and international and non-governmental organizations:

(a) Generate awareness of the disadvantaged situation of girls among policy makers, planners, administrators and implementors at all levels, as well as within households and communities;

(b) Make the girl child, particularly the girl child in difficult circumstances, aware of her own potential, educate her about the rights guaranteed to her under all international human rights instruments, including the Convention on the Rights of the Child, legislation enacted for her and the various measures undertaken by both governmental and non governmental organizations working to improve her status;

(c) Educate women, men, girls and boys to promote girls' status and encourage them to work towards mutual respect and equal partnership between girls and boys;

(d) Facilitate the equal provision of appropriate services and devices to girls with disabilities and provide their families with related support services, as appropriate.

STRATEGIC OBJECTIVE L.4.

> Eliminate discrimination against girls in education, skills development and training

---

Actions to be taken

279. By Governments:

(a) Ensure universal and equal access to and completion of primary education by all children and eliminate the existing gap between girls and boys, as stipulated in article 28 of the Convention on the Rights of the Child;[11] similarly, ensure equal access to secondary education by the year 2005 and equal access to higher education, including vocational and technical education, for all girls and boys, including the disadvantaged and gifted;

(b) Take steps to integrate functional literacy and numeracy programs, particularly for out-of-school girls in development programs; *(c)* Promote human rights education in educational programs and include in human rights edu-

cation the fact that the human rights of women and the girl child are an inalienable, integral and indivisible part of universal human rights;

(d) Increase enrollment and improve retention rates of girls by allocating appropriate budgetary resources and by enlisting the support of the community and parents through campaigns and flexible school schedules, incentives, scholarships, access programs for out-of-school girls and other measures;

(e) Develop training programs and materials for teachers and educators, raising awareness about their own role in the educational process, with a view to providing them with effective strategies for gender-sensitive teaching;

(f) Take actions to ensure that female teachers and professors have the same possibilities and status as male teachers and professors.

280. By Governments and international and non-governmental organizations:

(a) Provide education and skills training to increase girls' opportunities for employment and access to decision-making processes;

(b) Provide education to increase girls' knowledge and skills related to the functioning of economic, financial and political systems;

(c) Ensure access to appropriate education and skills-training for girl children with disabilities for their full participation in life;

(d) Promote the full and equal participation of girls in extracurricular activities, such as sports, drama and cultural activities.

STRATEGIC OBJECTIVE L. 5.

◆ Eliminate discrimination against girls in health and nutrition

Actions to be taken

281. By Governments and international and non-governmental organizations:

(a) Provide public information on the removal of discriminatory practices against girls in food allocation, nutrition and access to health services;

(b) Sensitize the girl child, parents, teachers and society concerning good general health and nutrition and raise awareness of the health dangers and other problems connected with early pregnancies;

(c) Strengthen and reorient health education and health services, particularly primary health care programs, including sexual and reproductive health, and design quality health programs that meet the physical and mental needs of girls and that attend to the needs of young, expectant and nursing mothers;

(d) Establish peer education and outreach programs with a view to strengthening individual and collective action to reduce the vulnerability of girls to HIV/AIDS and other sexually transmitted diseases, as agreed to in the Program of Action of the International Conference on Population and Devel-

opment and as established in the report of that Conference, recognizing the parental roles referred to in paragraph 267 of the present PLATFORM FOR ACTION ;

(e) Ensure education and dissemination of information to girls, especially adolescent girls, regarding the physiology of reproduction, reproductive and sexual health, as agreed to in the Program of Action of the International Conference on Population and Development and as established in the report of that Conference, responsible family planning practice, family life, reproductive health, sexually transmitted diseases, HIV infection and AIDS prevention, recognizing the parental roles referred to in paragraph 267;

(f) Include health and nutritional training as an integral part of literacy programs and school curricula starting at the primary level for the benefit of the girl child;

(g) Emphasize the role and responsibility of adolescents in sexual and reproductive health and behavior through the provision of appropriate services and counseling, as discussed in paragraph 267;

(h) Develop information and training programs for health planners and implements on the special health needs of the girl child;

(i) Take all the appropriate measures with a view to abolishing traditional practices prejudicial to the health of children, as stipulated in article 24 of the Convention on the Rights of the Child.[11]

STRATEGIC OBJECTIVE L. 6.

> *Eliminate the economic exploitation of child labor and protect young girls at work*

Actions to be taken

282. By Governments:

(a) In conformity with article 32 of the Convention on the Rights of the Child,[11] protect children from economic exploitation and from performing any work that is likely to be hazardous or to interfere with the child's education, or to be harmful to the child's health or physical, mental, spiritual, moral or social development;

(b) Define a minimum age for a child's admission to employment in national legislation, in conformity with existing international labor standards and the Convention on the Rights of the Child, including girls in all sectors of activity;

(c) Protect young girls at work, *inter alia*, through:

(i) A minimum age or ages for admission to employment;

(ii) Strict monitoring of work conditions (respect for work time, prohibition of work by children not provided for by national legislation, and monitoring of hygiene and health conditions at work);

(iii)Application of social security coverage;

(iv)Establishment of continuous training and education;

(d) Strengthen, where necessary, legislation governing the work of children and provide for appropriate penalties or other sanctions to ensure effective enforcement of the legislation;

(e) Use existing international labor standards, including, as appropriate, ILO standards for the protection of working children, to guide the formulation of national labor legislation and policies.

STRATEGIC OBJECTIVE L. 7.

❧ *Eradicate violence against the girl child*

Actions to be taken

283. By Governments and, as appropriate, international and non governmental organizations:

(a) Take effective actions and measures to enact and enforce legislation to protect the safety and security of girls from all forms of violence at work, including training programs and support programs, and take measures to eliminate incidents of sexual harassment of girls in educational and other institutions;

(b) Take appropriate legislative, administrative, social and educational measures to protect the girl child, in the household and in society, from all forms of physical or mental violence, injury or abuse, neglect or negligent treatment, maltreatment or exploitation, including sexual abuse;

(c) Undertake gender sensitization training for those involved in healing and rehabilitation and other assistance programs for girls who are victims of violence and promote programs of information, support and training for such girls;

(d) Enact and enforce legislation protecting girls from all forms of violence, including female infanticide and prenatal sex selection, genital mutilation, incest, sexual abuse, sexual exploitation, child prostitution and child pornography, and develop age-appropriate safe and confidential programs and medical, social and psychological support services to assist girls who are subjected to violence.

STRATEGIC OBJECTIVE L. 8.

❧ *Promote the girl child's awareness of and participation in social, economic and political life*

Actions to be taken

284. By Governments and international and non-governmental organizations:

(a) Provide access for girls to training, information and the media on social, cultural, economic and political issues and enable them to articulate their views;

(b) Support non-governmental organizations, in particular youth non governmental organizations, in their efforts to promote the equality and participation of girls in society.

STRATEGIC OBJECTIVE L. 9.

> ❧ *Strengthen the role of the family as defined in para. 29 above in improving the status of the girl child*

Actions to be taken

285. By Governments, in cooperation with non-governmental organizations:

(a) Formulate policies and programs to help the family, as defined in paragraph 29 above, in its supporting, educating and nurturing roles, with particular emphasis on the elimination of intra-family discrimination against the girl child;

(b) Provide an environment conducive to the strengthening of the family, as defined in paragraph 29 above, with a view to providing supportive and preventive measures which protect, respect and promote the potential of the girl child;

(c) Educate and encourage parents and caregivers to treat girls and boys equally and to ensure shared responsibilities between girls and boys in the family, as defined in paragraph 29 above.

Chapter V

Institutional Arrangements

286. The PLATFORM FOR ACTION establishes a set of actions that should lead to fundamental change. Immediate action and accountability are essential if the targets are to be met by the year 2000. Implementation is primarily the responsibility of Governments, but is also dependent on a wide range of institutions in the public, private and non-governmental sectors at the community, national, subregional/regional and international levels.

287. During the United Nations Decade for Women (1976-1985), many institutions specifically devoted to the advancement of women were established at the national, regional and international levels. At the international level, the International Research and Training Institute for the Advancement of Women (INSTRAW), the United Nations Development Fund for Women (UNIFEM), and the Committee to monitor the Convention on the Elimination of All Forms of Discrimination against Women were established. These entities, along with the Commission on the Status of Women and its secretariat, the Division for the Advancement of Women, became the main institutions in the United Nations specifically devoted to women's advancement globally. At the national level, a number of countries established or strengthened national mechanisms to plan, advocate for and monitor progress in the advancement of women.

288. Implementation of the PLATFORM FOR ACTION by national, subregional/regional and international institutions, both public and private, would be facilitated by transparency, by increased linkages between networks and organizations and by a consistent flow of information among all concerned. Clear objectives and accountability mechanisms are also required. Links with other institutions at the national, subregional/regional and international levels and with networks and organizations devoted to the advancement of women are needed.

289. Non-governmental and grass-roots organizations have a specific role to play in creating a social, economic, political and intellectual climate based on equality between women and men. Women should be actively involved in the implementation and monitoring of the PLATFORM FOR ACTION .

290. Effective implementation of the Platform will also require changes in the internal dynamics of institutions and organizations, including values, behavior, rules and procedures that are inimical to

the advancement of women. Sexual harassment should be eliminated.

291. National, subregional/regional and international institutions should have strong and clear mandates and the authority, resources and accountability mechanisms needed for the tasks set out in the PLATFORM FOR ACTION. Their methods of operation should ensure efficient and effective implementation of the Platform. There should be a clear commitment to international norms and standards of equality between women and men as a basis for all actions.

292. To ensure effective implementation of the PLATFORM FOR ACTION and to enhance the work for the advancement of women at the national, subregional/ regional and international levels, Governments, the United Nations system and all other relevant organizations should promote an active and visible policy of mainstreaming a gender perspective, *inter alia*, in the monitoring and evaluation of all policies and programs.

A. NATIONAL LEVEL

293. Governments have the primary responsibility for implementing the PLATFORM FOR ACTION. Commitment at the highest political level is essential to its implementation, and Governments should take a leading role in coordinating, monitoring and assessing progress in the advancement of women. The Fourth World Conference on Women is a conference of national and international commitment and action. This requires commitment from Governments and the international community. The PLATFORM FOR ACTION is part of a continuing process and has a catalytic effect as it will contribute to programs and practical outcomes for girls and women of all ages. States and the international community are encouraged to respond to this challenge by making commitments for action. As part of this process, many States have made commitments for action as reflected, *inter alia*, in their national statements.

294. National mechanisms and institutions for the advancement of women should participate in public policy formulation and encourage the implementation of the PLATFORM FOR ACTION through various bodies and institutions, including the private sector, and, where necessary, should act as a catalyst in developing new programs by the year 2000 in areas that are not covered by existing institutions.

295. The active support and participation of a broad and diverse range of other institutional actors should be encouraged, including legislative bodies, academic and research institutions, professional

associations, trade unions, cooperatives, local community groups, non-governmental organizations, including women's organizations and feminist groups, the media, religious groups, youth organizations and cultural groups, as well as financial and non-profit organizations.

296. In order for the PLATFORM FOR ACTION to be implemented, it will be necessary for Governments to establish or improve the effectiveness of national machineries for the advancement of women at the highest political level, appropriate intra- and inter-ministerial procedures and staffing, and other institutions with the mandate and capacity to broaden women's participation and integrate gender analysis into policies and programs. The first step in this process for all institutions should be to review their objectives, programs and operational procedures in terms of the actions called for in the Platform. A key activity should be to promote public awareness and support for the goals of the PLATFORM FOR ACTION, *inter alia*, through the mass media and public education.

297. As soon as possible, preferably by the end of 1995, Governments, in consultation with relevant institutions and non-governmental organizations, should begin to develop implementation strategies for the Platform and, preferably by the end of 1996, should have developed their strategies or plans of action. This planning process should draw upon persons at the highest level of authority in government and relevant actors in civil society. These implementation strategies should be comprehensive, have time-bound targets and benchmarks for monitoring, and include proposals for allocating or reallocating resources for implementation. Where necessary, the support of the international community could be enlisted, including resources.

298. Non-governmental organizations should be encouraged to contribute to the design and implementation of these strategies or national plans of action. They should also be encouraged to develop their own programs to complement government efforts. Women's organizations and feminist groups, in collaboration with other non-governmental organizations, should be encouraged to organize networks, as necessary, and to advocate for and support the implementation of the PLATFORM FOR ACTION by Governments and regional and international bodies.

299. Governments should commit themselves to gender balance, *inter alia*, through the creation of special mechanisms, in all government-appointed committees, boards and other relevant official bodies, as appropriate, as well as in all international bodies, institutions and organizations, notably by presenting and promoting more women candidates.

300. Regional and international organizations, in particular development institutions, especially INSTRAW, UNIFEM and bilateral donors, should provide financial and advisory assistance to national machinery in order to increase its ability to gather information, develop networks and carry out its mandate, in addition to strengthening international mechanisms to promote the advancement of women through their respective mandates, in cooperation with Governments.

B. SUBREGIONAL/REGIONAL LEVEL

301. The regional commissions of the United Nations and other subregional/ regional structures should promote and assist the pertinent national institutions in monitoring and implementing the global PLATFORM FOR ACTION within their mandates. This should be done in coordination with the implementation of the respective regional platforms or plans of action and in close collaboration with the Commission on the Status of Women, taking into account the need for a coordinated follow-up to United Nations conferences in the economic, social, human rights and related fields.

302. In order to facilitate the regional implementation, monitoring and evaluation process, the Economic and Social Council should consider reviewing the institutional capacity of the United Nations regional commissions within their mandates, including their women's units/focal points, to deal with gender issues in the light of the PLATFORM FOR ACTION, as well as the regional platforms and plans of action. Consideration should be given, *inter alia*, and, where appropriate, to strengthening capacity in this respect.

303. Within their existing mandates and activities, the regional commissions should mainstream women's issues and gender perspectives and should also consider the establishment of mechanisms and processes to ensure the implementation and monitoring of both the PLATFORM FOR ACTION and the regional platforms and plans of action. The regional commissions should, within their mandates, collaborate on gender issues with other regional intergovernmental organizations, non-governmental organizations, financial and research institutions and the private sector.

304. Regional offices of the specialized agencies of the United Nations system should, as appropriate, develop and publicize a plan of action for implementing the PLATFORM FOR ACTION, including the identification of time frames and resources. Technical assistance and operational activities at the regional level should establish well-

identified targets for the advancement of women. To this end, regular coordination should be undertaken among United Nations bodies and agencies.

305. Non-governmental organizations within the region should be supported in their efforts to develop networks to coordinate advocacy and dissemination of information about the global PLATFORM FOR ACTION and the respective regional platforms or plans of action.

C. INTERNATIONAL LEVEL

1. United Nations

306. The PLATFORM FOR ACTION needs to be implemented through the work of all of the bodies and organizations of the United Nations system during the period 1995-2000, specifically and as an integral part of wider programming. An enhanced framework for international cooperation for gender issues must be developed during the period 1995-2000 in order to ensure the integrated and comprehensive implementation, follow-up and assessment of the PLATFORM FOR ACTION, taking into account the results of global United Nations summits and conferences. The fact that at all of these summits and conferences, Governments have committed themselves to the empowerment of women in different areas, makes coordination crucial to the follow-up strategies for this PLATFORM FOR ACTION. The Agenda for Development and the Agenda for Peace should take into account the PLATFORM FOR ACTION of the Fourth World Conference on Women.

307. The institutional capacity of the United Nations system to carry out and coordinate its responsibility for implementing the PLATFORM FOR ACTION, as well as its expertise and working methods to promote the advancement of women, should be improved.

308. Responsibility for ensuring the implementation of the PLATFORM FOR ACTION and the integration of a gender perspective into all policies and programs of the United Nations system must rest at the highest levels.

309. To improve the system's efficiency and effectiveness in providing support for equality and women's empowerment at the national level and to enhance its capacity to achieve the objectives of the PLATFORM FOR ACTION, there is a need to renew, reform and revitalize various parts of the United Nations system. This would include reviewing and strengthening the strategies and working methods of different United Nations mechanisms for the advancement of women with a view to rationalizing and, as appropriate, strengthen-

ing their advisory, catalytic and monitoring functions in relation to mainstream bodies and agencies. Women/gender units are important for effective mainstreaming, but strategies must be further developed to prevent inadvertent marginalization as opposed to mainstreaming of the gender dimension throughout all operations.

310. In following up the Fourth World Conference on Women, all entities of the United Nations system focusing on the advancement of women should have the necessary resources and support to carry out follow-up activities. The efforts of gender focal points within organizations should be well integrated into overall policy, planning, programming and budgeting.

311. Action must be taken by the United Nations and other international organizations to eliminate barriers to the advancement of women within their organizations in accordance with the PLATFORM FOR ACTION.

General Assembly

312. The General Assembly, as the highest intergovernmental body in the United Nations, is the principal policy-making and appraisal organ on matters relating to the follow-up to the Conference, and as such, should integrate gender issues throughout its work. It should appraise progress in the effective implementation of the PLATFORM FOR ACTION, recognizing that these issues cut across social, political and economic policy. At its fiftieth session, in 1995, the General Assembly will have before it the report of the Fourth World Conference on Women. In accordance with its resolution 49/161, it will also examine a report of the Secretary-General on the follow-up to the Conference, taking into account the recommendations of the Conference. The General Assembly should include the follow-up to the Conference as part of its continuing work on the advancement of women. In 1996, 1998 and 2000, it should review the implementation of the PLATFORM FOR ACTION.

Economic and Social Council

313. The Economic and Social Council, in the context of its role under the Charter of the United Nations and in accordance with General Assembly resolutions 45/264, 46/235 and 48/162, would oversee system-wide coordination in the implementation of the PLATFORM FOR ACTION and make recommendations in this regard. The Council should be invited to review the implementation of the PLATFORM FOR ACTION, giving due consideration to the reports of the Commission on the Status of Women. As coordinating body, the Council should be invited to review the mandate of the Commission on the Status of Women, taking into account the need for effective coordination with other related commissions and Confer-

ence follow-up. The Council should incorporate gender issues into its discussion of all policy questions, giving due consideration to recommendations prepared by the Commission. It should consider dedicating at least one high-level segment before the year 2000 to the advancement of women and implementation of the PLATFORM FOR ACTION with the active involvement and participation, *inter alia*, of the specialized agencies, including the World Bank and IMF.

314. The Council should consider dedicating at least one coordination segment before the year 2000 to coordination of the advancement of women, based on the revised system-wide medium-term plan for the advancement of women.

315. The Council should consider dedicating at least one operational activities segment before the year 2000 to the coordination of development activities related to gender, based on the revised system-wide medium-term plan for the advancement of women, with a view to instituting guidelines and procedures for implementation of the PLATFORM FOR ACTION by the funds and programs of the United Nations system.

316. The Administrative Committee on Coordination (ACC) should consider how its participating entities might best coordinate their activities, *inter alia*, through existing procedures at the inter-agency level for ensuring system-wide coordination to implement and help follow up the objectives of the PLATFORM FOR ACTION .

- COMMISSION ON THE STATUS OF WOMEN

317. The General Assembly and the Economic and Social Council, in accordance with their respective mandates, are invited to review and strengthen the mandate of the Commission on the Status of Women, taking into account the PLATFORM FOR ACTION as well as the need for synergy with other related commissions and Conference follow-up, and for a system-wide approach to its implementation.

318. As a functional commission assisting the Economic and Social Council, the Commission on the Status of Women should have a central role in monitoring, within the United Nations system, the implementation of the PLATFORM FOR ACTION and advising the Council thereon. It should have a clear mandate with sufficient human and financial resources, through the reallocation of resources within the regular budget of the United Nations to carry the mandate out.

319. The Commission on the Status of Women should assist the Economic and Social Council in its coordination of the reporting on the implementation of the PLATFORM FOR ACTION with the relevant organizations of the United Nations system. The Commission

should draw upon inputs from other organizations of the United Nations system and other sources, as appropriate.

320. The Commission on the Status of Women, in developing its work program for the period 1996-2000, should review the critical areas of concern in the PLATFORM FOR ACTION and consider how to integrate in its agenda the follow-up to the World Conference on Women. In this context, the Commission on the Status of Women could consider how it could further develop its catalytic role in mainstreaming a gender perspective in United Nations activities.

Other functional commissions

321. Within their mandates, other functional commissions of the Economic and Social Council should also take due account of the PLATFORM FOR ACTION and ensure the integration of gender aspects in their respective work.

- COMMITTEE ON THE ELIMINATION OF DISCRIMINATION AGAINST WOMEN and other treaty bodies

322. The Committee on the Elimination of Discrimination against Women, in implementing its responsibilities under the Convention on the Elimination of All Forms of Discrimination against Women, should, within its mandate, take into account the PLATFORM FOR ACTION when considering the reports submitted by States parties.

323. States parties to the Convention on the Elimination of All Forms of Discrimination against Women are invited, when reporting under article 18 of the Convention, to include information on measures taken to implement the PLATFORM FOR ACTION in order to facilitate the Committee on the Elimination of Discrimination against Women in monitoring effectively women's ability to enjoy the rights guaranteed by the Convention.

324. The ability of the Committee on the Elimination of Discrimination against Women to monitor implementation of the Convention should be strengthened through the provision of human and financial resources within the regular budget of the United Nations, including expert legal assistance and, in accordance with General Assembly resolution 49/164 and the decision made by the meeting of States parties to the Convention held in May 1995, sufficient meeting time for the Committee. The Committee should increase its coordination with other human rights treaty bodies, taking into account the recommendations in the Vienna Declaration and Program of Action.

325. Within their mandate, other treaty bodies should also take due account of the implementation of the PLATFORM FOR ACTION and ensure the integration of the equal status and human rights of women in their work.

United Nations Secretariat

- OFFICE OF THE SECRETARY-GENERAL

326. The Secretary-General is requested to assume responsibility for coordination of policy within the United Nations for the implementation of the PLATFORM FOR ACTION and for the mainstreaming of a system-wide gender perspective in all activities of the United Nations, taking into account the mandates of the bodies concerned. The Secretary-General should consider specific measures for ensuring effective coordination in the implementation of these objectives. To this end, the Secretary-General is invited to establish a high-level post in the office of the Secretary- General, using existing human and financial resources, to act as the Secretary-General's adviser on gender issues and to help ensure system-wide implementation of the PLATFORM FOR ACTION in close cooperation with the Division for the Advancement of Women.

- DIVISION FOR THE ADVANCEMENT OF WOMEN

327. The primary function of the Division for the Advancement of Women of the Department for Policy Coordination and Sustainable Development is to provide substantive servicing to the Commission on the Status of Women and other intergovernmental bodies when they are concerned with the advancement of women, as well as to the Committee on the Elimination of Discrimination against Women. It has been designated a focal point for the implementation of the Nairobi *Forward-looking Strategies for the Advancement of Women*. In the light of the review of the mandate of the Commission on the Status of Women, as set out in paragraph 313 above, the functions of the Division for the Advancement of Women will also need to be assessed. The Secretary- General is requested to ensure more effective functioning of the Division by, *inter alia*, providing sufficient human and financial resources within the regular budget of the United Nations.

328. The Division should examine the obstacles to the advancement of women through the application of gender-impact analysis in policy studies for the Commission on the Status of Women and through support to other subsidiary bodies. After the Fourth World Conference on Women it should play a coordinating role in preparing the revision of the system-wide medium-term plan for the advancement of women for the period 1996-2001 and should continue serving as the secretariat for inter-agency coordination for the advancement of women. It should continue to maintain a flow of information with national commissions, national institutions for the advancement of women and non-governmental organizations with regard to implementation of the PLATFORM FOR ACTION.

Other units of the United Nations Secretariat

329. The various units of the United Nations Secretariat should examine their programs to determine how they can best contribute to the coordinated implementation of the PLATFORM FOR ACTION. Proposals for implementation of the Platform need to be reflected in the revision of the system-wide medium-term plan for the advancement of women for the period 1996-2001, as well as in the proposed United Nations medium-term plan for the period 1998-2002. The content of the actions will depend on the mandates of the bodies concerned.

330. Existing and new linkages should be developed throughout the-Secretariat in order to ensure that the gender perspective is introduced as a central dimension in all activities of the Secretariat.

331. The Office of Human Resources Management should, in collaboration with program managers world wide, and in accordance with the strategic plan of action for the improvement of the status of women in the Secretariat (1995-2000), continue to accord priority to the recruitment and promotion of women in posts subject to geographical distribution, particularly in senior policy-level and decision-making posts, in order to achieve the goals set out in General Assembly resolutions 45/125 and 45/239 C and reaffirmed in General Assembly resolutions 46/100, 47/93, 48/106 and 49/167. The training service should design and conduct regular gender sensitivity training or include gender sensitivity training in all of its activities.

332. The Department of Public Information should seek to integrate a gender perspective in its general information activities and, within existing resources, strengthen and improve its programs on women and the girl child. To this end, the Department should formulate a multimedia communications strategy to support the implementation of the PLATFORM FOR ACTION, taking new technology fully into account. Regular outputs of the Department should promote the goals of the Platform, particularly in developing countries.

333. The Statistical Division of the Department for Economic and Social Information and Policy Analysis should have an important coordinating role in international work in statistics, as described above in chapter IV, strategic objective H.3.

- INTERNATIONAL RESEARCH AND TRAINING INSTITUTE FOR THE ADVANCEMENT OF WOMEN

334. INSTRAW has a mandate to promote research and training on women's situation and development. In the light of the PLATFORM FOR ACTION, INSTRAW should review its work program and develop a program for implementing those aspects of the PLATFORM

FOR ACTION that fall within its mandate. It should identify those types of research and research methodologies to be given priority, strengthen national capacities to carry out women's studies and gender research, including that on the status of the girl child, and develop networks of research institutions that can be mobilized for that purpose. It should also identify those types of education and training that can be effectively supported and promoted by the Institute.

- UNITED NATIONS DEVELOPMENT FUND FOR WOMEN

335. UNIFEM has the mandate to increase options and opportunities for women's economic and social development in developing countries by providing technical and financial assistance to incorporate the women's dimension into development at all levels. Therefore, UNIFEM should review and strengthen, as appropriate, its work program in the light of the PLATFORM FOR ACTION, focusing on women's political and economic empowerment. Its advocacy role should concentrate on fostering a multilateral policy dialogue on women's empowerment. Adequate resources for carrying out its functions should be made available.

Specialized agencies and other organizations of the United Nations system

336. To strengthen their support for actions at the national level and to enhance their contributions to coordinated follow-up by the United Nations, each organization should set out the specific actions they will undertake, including goals and targets to realign priorities and redirect resources to meet the global priorities identified in the PLATFORM FOR ACTION. There should be a clear delineation of responsibility and accountability. These proposals should in turn be reflected in the system-wide medium-term plan for the advancement of women for the period 1996-2001.

337. Each organization should commit itself at the highest level and, in pursuing its targets, should take steps to enhance and support the roles and responsibilities of its focal points on women's issues.

338. In addition, specialized agencies with mandates to provide technical assistance in developing countries, particularly in Africa and the least developed countries, should cooperate more to ensure the continuing promotion of the advancement of women.

339. The United Nations system should consider and provide appropriate technical assistance and other forms of assistance to the countries with economies in transition in order to facilitate solution of their specific problems regarding the advancement of women.

340. Each organization should accord greater priority to the recruitment and promotion of women at the Professional level to achieve

gender balance, particularly at decision-making levels. The paramount consideration in the employment of the staff and in the determination of the conditions of service should be the necessity of securing the highest standards of efficiency, competence and integrity. Due regard should be paid to the importance of recruiting the staff on as wide a geographical basis as possible. Organizations should report regularly to their governing bodies on progress towards this goal.

341. Coordination of United Nations operational activities for development at the country level should be improved through the resident coordinator system in accordance with relevant resolutions of the General Assembly, in particular General Assembly resolution 47/199, to take full account of the PLATFORM FOR ACTION.

2. Other international institutions and organizations

342. In implementing the PLATFORM FOR ACTION, international financial institutions are encouraged to review and revise policies, procedures and staffing to ensure that investments and programs benefit women and thus contribute to sustainable development. They are also encouraged to increase the number of women in high-level positions, increase staff training in gender analysis and institute policies and guidelines to ensure full consideration of the differential impact of lending programs and other activities on women and men. In this regard, the Bretton Woods institutions, the United Nations, as well as its funds and programs and the specialized agencies, should establish regular and substantive dialogue, including dialogue at the field level, for more efficient and effective coordination of their assistance in order to strengthen the effectiveness of their programs for the benefit of women and their families.

343. The General Assembly should give consideration to inviting the World Trade Organization to consider how it might contribute to the implementation of the PLATFORM FOR ACTION, including activities in cooperation with the United Nations system.

344. International non-governmental organizations have an important role to play in implementing the PLATFORM FOR ACTION. Consideration should be given to establishing a mechanism for collaborating with non-governmental organizations to promote the implementation of the Platform at various levels.

Chapter VI

Financial Arrangements

345. Financial and human resources have generally been insufficient for the advancement of women. This has contributed to the slow progress to date in implementing the Nairobi *Forward-looking Strategies for the Advancement of Women*. Full and effective implementation of the PLATFORM FOR ACTION, including the relevant commitments made at previous United Nations summits and conferences, will require a political commitment to make available human and financial resources for the empowerment of women. This will require the integration of a gender perspective in budgetary decisions on policies and programs, as well as the adequate financing of specific programs for securing equality between women and men. To implement the PLATFORM FOR ACTION, funding will need to be identified and mobilized from all sources and across all sectors. The reformulation of policies and reallocation of resources may be needed within and among programs, but some policy changes may not necessarily have financial implications. Mobilization of additional resources, both public and private, including resources from innovative sources of funding, may also be necessary.

A. NATIONAL LEVEL

346. The primary responsibility for implementing the strategic objectives of the PLATFORM FOR ACTION rests with Governments. To achieve these objectives, Governments should make efforts to systematically review how women benefit from public sector expenditures; adjust budgets to ensure equality of access to public sector expenditures, both for enhancing productive capacity and for meeting social needs; and achieve the gender related commitments made in other United Nations summits and conferences. To develop successful national implementation strategies for the PLATFORM FOR ACTION, Governments should allocate sufficient resources, including resources for undertaking gender-impact analysis. Governments should also encourage non-governmental organizations and private-sector and other institutions to mobilize additional resources.

347. Sufficient resources should be allocated to national machineries for the advancement of women as well as to all institutions, as ap-

propriate, that can contribute to the implementation and monitoring of the PLATFORM FOR ACTION.

348. Where national machineries for the advancement of women do not yet exist or where they have not yet been established on a permanent basis, Governments should strive to make available sufficient and continuing resources for such machineries.

349. To facilitate the implementation of the PLATFORM FOR ACTION, Governments should reduce, as appropriate, excessive military expenditures and investments for arms production and acquisition, consistent with national security requirements.

350. Non-governmental organizations, the private sector and other actors of civil society should be encouraged to consider allocating the resources necessary for the implementation of the PLATFORM FOR ACTION. Governments should create a supportive environment for the mobilization of resources by non-governmental organizations, particularly women's organizations and networks, feminist groups, the private sector and other actors of civil society, to enable them to contribute towards this end. The capacity of non-governmental organizations in this regard should be strengthened and enhanced.

B. REGIONAL LEVEL

351. Regional development banks, regional business associations and other regional institutions should be invited to contribute to and help mobilize resources in their lending and other activities for the implementation of the PLATFORM FOR ACTION. They should also be encouraged to take account of the PLATFORM FOR ACTION in their policies and funding modalities.

352. The subregional and regional organizations and the United Nations regional commissions should, where appropriate and within their existing mandates, assist in the mobilization of funds for the implementation of the PLATFORM FOR ACTION.

C. INTERNATIONAL LEVEL

353. Adequate financial resources should be committed at the international level for the implementation of the PLATFORM FOR ACTION in the developing countries, particularly in Africa and the least developed countries. Strengthening national capacities in developing

countries to implement the PLATFORM FOR ACTION will require striving for the fulfillment of the agreed target of 0.7 per cent of the gross national product of developed countries for overall official development assistance as soon as possible, as well as increasing the share of funding for activities designed to implement the PLATFORM FOR ACTION. Furthermore, countries involved in development cooperation should conduct a critical analysis of their assistance programs so as to improve the quality and effectiveness of aid through the integration of a gender approach.

354. International financial institutions, including the World Bank, the International Monetary Fund, the International Fund for Agricultural Development and the regional development banks, should be invited to examine their grants and lending and to allocate loans and grants to programs for implementing the PLATFORM FOR ACTION in developing countries, especially in Africa and the least developed countries.

355. The United Nations system should provide technical cooperation and other forms of assistance to the developing countries, in particular in Africa and the least developed countries, in implementing the PLATFORM FOR ACTION.

356. Implementation of the PLATFORM FOR ACTION in the countries with economies in transition will require continued international cooperation and assistance. The organizations and bodies of the United Nations system, including the technical and sectoral agencies, should facilitate the efforts of those countries in designing and implementing policies and programs for the advancement of women. To this end, the International Monetary Fund and the World Bank should be invited to assist those efforts.

357. The outcome of the World Summit for Social Development regarding debt management and reduction as well as other United Nations world summits and conferences should be implemented in order to facilitate the realization of the objectives of the PLATFORM FOR ACTION.

358. To facilitate implementation of the PLATFORM FOR ACTION, interested developed and developing country partners, agreeing on a mutual commitment to allocate, on average, 20 per cent of official development assistance and 20 per cent of the national budget to basic social programs should take into account a gender perspective.

359. Development funds and programs of the United Nations system should undertake an immediate analysis of the extent to which their programs and projects are directed to implementing the PLATFORM FOR ACTION and, for the next programming cycle, should ensure the

adequacy of resources targeted towards eliminating disparities between women and men in their technical assistance and funding activities.

360. Recognizing the roles of United Nations funds, programs and specialized agencies, in particular the special roles of UNIFEM and INSTRAW, in the promotion of the empowerment of women, and therefore in the implementation of the PLATFORM FOR ACTION within their respective mandates, *inter alia*, in research, training and information activities for the advancement of women as well as technical and financial assistance to incorporate a gender perspective in development efforts, the resources provided by the international community need to be sufficient and should be maintained at an adequate level.

361. To improve the efficiency and effectiveness of the United Nations system in its efforts to promote the advancement of women and to enhance its capacity to further the objectives of the PLATFORM FOR ACTION, there is a need to renew, reform and revitalize various parts of the United Nations system, especially the Division for the Advancement of Women of the United Nations Secretariat, as well as other units and subsidiary bodies that have a specific mandate to promote the advancement of women. In this regard, relevant governing bodies within the United Nations system are encouraged to give special consideration to the effective implementation of the PLATFORM FOR ACTION and to review their policies, programs, budgets and activities in order to achieve the most effective and efficient use of funds to this end. Allocation of additional resources from within the United Nations regular budget in order to implement the PLATFORM FOR ACTION will also be necessary.

Notes

1. *Report of the World Conference to Review and Appraise the Achievements of the United Nations Decade for Women: Equality, Development and Peace*, Nairobi, 15-26 July 1985 (United Nations publication, Sales No. E.85.IV.10),chap.I,sect.A.

2. *Report of the World Conference on Human Rights*, Vienna, 14-25 June 1993 (A/CONF.157/24 (Part I)), chap. III.

3. General Assembly resolution 34/180, annex.

4. General Assembly resolution 45/164.

5. General Assembly resolution 44/82.

6. General Assembly resolution 48/126. 7/ A/47/308-E/1992/97, annex.

8. General Assembly resolution 48/104.

9. *Vienna Declaration and Program of Action, Report of the World Conference on Human Rights*. chap. III, para. 5.

10. See *The Results of the Uruguay Round of Multilateral Trade Negotiations: The Legal Texts* (Geneva, GATT secretariat, 1994).

11. General Assembly resolution 44/25, annex.

12. *Final Report of the World Conference on Education for All: Meeting Basic Learning Needs*, Jomtien, Thailand, 5-9 March 1990, Inter-Agency Commission (UNDP, UNESCO, UNICEF, World Bank) for the World Conference on Education for All, New York, 1990, appendix 1.

13. General Assembly resolution 2200 A (XXI), annex.

14. *Report of the International Conference on Population and Development*, Cairo, 5-13 September 1994 (United Nations publication, Sales No. E.95.XIII.18), chap. I, resolution 1, annex.

15. *Report of the World Summit for Social Development*, Copenhagen, 6-12 March 1995 (A/CONF.166/9), chap. I, resolution 1, annexes I and II.

16. Unsafe abortion is defined as a procedure for terminating an unwanted pregnancy either by persons lacking the necessary skills or in an environment lacking the minimal medical standards or both (based on World Health Organization, *The Prevention and Management of Unsafe Abortion, Report of a Technical Working Group*, Geneva, April 1992 (WHO/MSM/92.5)).

17. *Final Report of the International Conference on Nutrition*, Rome, 511 December 1992 (Rome, Food and Agriculture Organization of the United Nations, 1993), Part II.

18. *Report of the United Nations Conference on Environment and Development*, Rio de Janeiro, 3-14 June 1992, vol. I, Resolutions Adopted by the Conference (United Nations publication, Sales No. E.93.I.8 and corrigenda), resolution 1, annex I.

19. Ibid., resolution 1, annex II.

20. General Assembly resolution 317 (IV), annex.

21. General Assembly resolution 217 A (III).

22. General Assembly resolution 39/46, annex.

23. *Official Records of the General Assembly*, Forty-seventh Session, Supplement No. 38 (A/47/38), chap. I.

24. United Nations, *Treaty Series*, vol. 75, No. 973, p. 287.

25. *Report of the World Conference on Human Rights*. chap. III, sect. II, para. 38.

26. See *The United Nations Disarmament Yearbook*, vol. 5: 1980 (United Nations publication, Sales No. E.81.IX.4), appendix VII.

27. General Assembly resolution 260 A (III), annex.

28. United Nations, *Treaty Series*, vol. 189, No. 2545.

29. Ibid., vol. 606, No. 8791.

30. General Assembly resolution 48/96, annex.

31. General Assembly resolution 1386 (XIV).

32. See CEDAW/SP/1995/2.

33. General Assembly resolution 2106 A (XX), annex.

34. General Assembly resolution 41/128, annex.

35. United Nations Environment Program, *Convention on Biological Diversity* (Environmental Law and Institutions Program Activity Center), June 1992.